# THE
# FAROES
# VENTURE

# THE FAROES VENTURE

*Jeremy Lucas*

JONATHAN CAPE
THIRTY-TWO BEDFORD SQUARE
LONDON

First published 1987
Copyright © 1987 by Jeremy Lucas
Jonathan Cape Ltd, 32 Bedford Square, London WC1B 3EL

British Library Cataloguing in Publication Data
Lucas, Jeremy
The Faroes venture.
I. Title
823′.914 [F]          PR6062. U14/

ISBN 0–224–02458–2

Typeset at The Spartan Press Ltd,
Lymington, Hants
Printed in Great Britain by
Robert Hartnoll (1985) Ltd,
Bodmin, Cornwall

# *Preface*

This is a story of whaling, *the* high adventure of our times. The scene has been set in that area of the North Atlantic where whaling is practised in the most bloody and ruthless way: in the waters of the Faroe Islands. I must stress that although the killing and the methods described in these pages are what really happens, the names given to the actors in this story are very frequently to be found in the Faroes or in Denmark and the characters described bear no resemblance at all to any person, living or dead.

I have been exact in my descriptions of traditional pilot whale hunting and Norwegian-style finback whaling, aided by extensive observations in the Atlantic Ocean. Some of the resultant imagery, therefore, is harsh.

It should also be made clear that the Faroese generally, despite whatever picture the media has misguidedly created over the past five years, are a strong, kind people, essentially Scandinavian in character, though enriched with their own culture and extraordinary history. As in any nation in the world, however, there are powerful elements present which are totally evil.

The visitor to this lonely archipelago, just two hundred miles south of the Arctic Circle, will be astounded by its overwhelming beauty; and yet, because of its remote location and capricious climate, it receives few tourists. I have included endpaper maps which can be followed throughout the story. I have used Faroese place names, including their proper alphabetical representation, throughout the text, giving the English translation where the meaning reveals something of the area's nature. One peculiarity of the language which should be highlighted is the letter ð. It is usually pronounced th as in the English word with, but much more highly aspirated.

The Faroese tongue, particularly its pronunciation, is complicated, made more so by a wide spectrum of both vowel and consonant sounds. Faroese belongs to the Norse group of languages, bearing closest resemblance to Icelandic and certain Norwegian dialects. For those readers who might be interested in learning the rudiments of this enchanting language, *An Introduction to Modern Faroese*, by W. B. Lockwood is outstanding. The book is published by Føroya Skúlabókagrunnur, Tórshavn, Faroe Islands.

A final point concerning pronunciation, of relevance to this story, is of the Danish name Claus, which is spoken just as Klaus in German, *not* as the English pronounce the name in Santa Claus.

I am indebted to many friends at, or formerly at, King's College, London University, for technical guidance concerning some of the machinery and apparatus described in these pages. My thanks also to Alan Thornton, Director of the Environmental Investigation Agency Limited, for early research material. Special thanks are due to all those natives of the Faroe Islands who made me welcome or explained to me various aspects of life on the islands; Hans Hermansen, Helena Dam and Eidi Nielsen of Tórshavn; the staff of Føroya Landsbókasavn who directed me to incredibly detailed and fascinating historical records, unavailable in Europe; Kjartan Hoydal, Director of Fisheries; Claus and Jens Hansen, my Danish companions who were known as my 'bodyguards' and who took me through the bad time; the fishermen Jákup, Peter and Ongur at Vestmanna and Klaksvík; the whalers, Jóannes and Rikard, and Björn the 'mad Norwegian'. To all of these I promised to tell the truth, in novel form, of how it is on the Faroes. I have done that and hope to have corrected some of the nonsense written by the journalists who I was ashamed to admit were my fellow countrymen. But, as I explained to them all, I have not disguised the bloody details of the whaling. It cannot, and should not, be disguised.

Most of all I thank my wife, Katharine, who has suffered my various moods, and my absence in the Faroes, as I developed, researched and wrote the story. This book is dedicated to her.

1987                                                          JL

1     The Greenlanders were in port, so no one spoke
too loudly. The café was quiet, despite the number of fishing
vessels moored up in the harbour and everyone drinking too
much, far into the deep winter night. The Greenlanders drank
most of all; vodka from the Russian trawlers, swapped for fish
on the high seas. Wary eyes glanced at the dark, flat-faced men,
the Eskimos, the people who betrayed no warmth to their souls,
like the hard, high land which was their home.

No one dared stare too long, in case their glance was caught
and taken the wrong way. You showed respect for a Greenland
fisherman or cargo worker, you kept your distance and laughed
only when he laughed louder, and you never upset him with the
wrong sort of stare. You remembered that only an Eskimo could
slash a spear across the fugitive target of a salmon's flank as the
fish sped into fresh water from the sea. And if you had imagination you believed the strange stories, and you were careful.

The café was filling with customers as more boats tied up for
the bitter night. Tobacco smoke thickened the air while the
murmur became a chatter and the Greenlanders became very
drunk. Men were discarding their furs and oilskins as a steamy,
salty heat enveloped the place. The atmosphere could not have
been that of any other northern ocean harbour where fishermen
and freightermen gathered in winter; not Bergen, St John's or
Stornoway, not even Rejkyavik. This was Tórshavn, Faroe
Islands, a lonely outpost for seafarers in the north-eastern
Atlantic. Beyond, away from the islands in any direction for
hundreds of miles, lay the wild, winter sea, and men's fears.

Claus Hansen, the tall Danish smuggler, drank some more whisky and enjoyed the marvellous warmth. He smiled to himself as he thought briefly of the last run the night before; the way he had pushed *Hannah* through the reefs off Suduroy in a half storm, off-loaded his cargo to the waiting boats in Hvalbiarfjord, and run back out into the night. Only five islanders knew he had been there, and they would not talk.

To most people Claus was what he appeared to be, a fisherman who occasionally brought in a load from Esbjerg. Some suspected he was a renegade, who maybe ran a little illicit cargo, but he had never been caught and no one had had the bad taste to ask. The Greenlanders knew, without being told. They knew just by looking at him. Something in the angular, Norse looks of the man told them; the intense blue, yet not cold, eyes, the coolness of his personality. They respected him, even though he was not of their kind. Some had asked him to run whisky out of Scotland, and he had refused. Claus did not smuggle alcohol.

The Faroese in the café were getting noisy now, even though the Greenlanders were still awake. With the alcohol rationing on the islands the residents became drunk for days on end when the fishing boats brought in cases of spirits. Claus shrugged. They were stupid, organising their lives around the next bottle, happy only when they had a drink. And those who brought the stuff in, selling it at up to ten times its market value, were bad men, so Claus thought, whether they were Canadians, Danes or Eskimos. There were better things to run; electrical goods, clothes, even the occasional motor cycle. You never made the same profits as with alcohol, and it was more dangerous; but it was *good* smuggling.

He could not hear the wind any more above the laughing and shouting. There would be a dance soon and then a fight, and someone would end up in the water. It would not be him. No one had picked a fight with him for ten years, or thrown him in the water for twenty. He refused to become involved in their ridiculous arguments. To them he was an enigma, and therefore dangerous, but, anyway, most of them liked him.

Most, but not all. Jákup Poulsen, the whaler, did not like him; not since the day that Claus had used *Hannah* to turn two big finbacks out to sea, and then guarded them until Poulsen's harpoon boat, *Stormur*, could not continue the chase. Jákup, hunched now over a dozen empty bottles of beer, was watching his old enemy, feeling the old bitterness in his stomach, and the intense hatred for the Dane. Most of all he wondered how one day he would take his revenge – kill him, or, at least, set him up with the Authorities.

Sitting at Jákup's table were the crew-members of his boat, all Faroese except for the mad engineer, who was Icelandic. They too disliked the Dane, but only because their captain did so. Claus knew they were all looking at him, and ignored them. The only one who was man enough to start anything was Jákup, the others were worms. He was enjoying the noise and the warmth. The whalers did not worry him, not while the Greenlanders were around, and with Jens, his own crew-man, back on board *Hannah*.

Here, in the anonymity of the café, he could think. He wondered how the Englishman would take all this, whether he would cope with the strange mixture of northern cultures which made up the Faroes, and whether he would be brave enough to take on these people, and these seas, with his adventurous idea. Was the Englishman trying for too much? He did not know the Faroese, even if he adequately understood the North Atlantic. He would need so much of Claus's help and knowledge. It would not be long now, for it was already March and winter was nearly over. He would have to bring the Englishman in during the early summer, May perhaps, and then if all went well – Claus smiled openly and looked across at the whalers –Jákup Poulsen would not know what hit him.

Some adventure anyway, and Claus liked adventure.

He stood and buttoned his heavy coat. Jákup saw him and shouted across the café. 'Are you leaving, bastard Dane, before we can have some fun, eh?'

Claus, still smiling, walked across to the table, carrying with him a half-empty bottle of whisky. When he reached where the

11

Faroese captain was sitting he stooped down to speak in his ear, putting a hand on his shoulder. 'Ya, bastard Føroyingur, I'm leaving now. But one day we meet out there, eh, on the water, and we have some fun.' The mad engineer stood up and raised his arm, until Claus caught it. 'Na, na, na, you would not like the Eskimos to see you do that. Sit down and have another drink; spoil your brain a little more.' He pushed the Icelander heavily back into the chair. None of the others was drunk enough yet to start a fight, at least before there had been some dancing, or some of the Greenlanders were asleep.

'You like trouble too much,' said Jákup evenly. 'One day you'll make a big mistake; and I think perhaps I'll be there to see you make it. Like,' he continued slowly, 'if ever you are again between me and a whale I swear I'll fire a hot harpoon below your waterline.'

'Maybe.' Claus sniffed and turned towards the door. So many of these seafarers needed trouble, as if the Atlantic did not give them enough. Men never learnt, no matter what happened, and so there was no hope, really. But you had to try, and had to make your statement, to stop your own world becoming as rotten as theirs. And you needed courage. More than anything else in that northern maelstrom of wind and water and violence and ignorance, you needed courage.

She stood in the half-light thrown from the kiosk by the café, where Claus had known she would be. The wind had dropped but it was still cold and a mist was descending over the harbour.

'You will be cold, Eidi,' he said to her. Out there, apart from the murmur seeping from the café and the tide slopping against the hulls of ships, it was strangely quiet, as before a storm. 'Have you been waiting long?' She did not answer as he ran a hand over her cold cheeks. 'You must come to the boat. It's warm there.'

Through the shadows they walked along the quayside. They felt alone in Tórshavn, alone on the lava mass that was the Faroes. They shared their thoughts without speech, for they

12

had learned to understand one another during the rare, treasured moments they had stolen together over the ten years that Claus had fished and smuggled in Faroese waters.

At twenty-six Eidi felt alone in the world, except during those times she shared with Claus. Her parents were dead and she had few friends, being avoided by the men of the islands in spite of her beauty, for she had a ruthless protector; her brother, Jákup Poulsen.

At last, as they approached the *Hannah*, Eidi spoke. 'He was there.' It was not a question.

'You must not worry about him. He likes to make trouble for people.'

'He hates you. He will make as much trouble for you as he is able.'

'In every harbour is a man like your brother. They do not frighten me. I know how to handle them, and their henchmen. I cannot run away from them. If I were to fear such men, I could not see the beauty that lies beyond them. Then I would fear life itself, as they do.'

'But you must be careful.'

'Always, Eidi. For your sake I will be careful.'

They stepped on board over *Hannah*'s curved wooden gunwhale. As they climbed down from the wheelhouse they heard a girl giggling. Claus banged on the door of his crewman's cabin and shouted. 'Jens, you dog, Jákup is around. I do not think he will give us problems tonight, but I want you to listen for anyone on deck.'

There was a grunt of acknowledgment followed by more giggling. Then Claus and Eidi were inside the wooden cocoon of his own cabin. Jens would listen, no matter how much fun he was having. And Eidi felt safe and happy for the first time in two months, since the last smuggling run.

Later that night, just before dawn, a big storm broke from the north-west, howling down out of Icelandic waters. Claus knew that the blow would trap him in Tórshavn until it passed, and it would probably last a week. He also knew that it was winter's final real attack. After the storm it would be spring.

The tjaldur, oyster-catchers, would arrive and the days begin to lengthen. That would be good, to escape the long, gale-blown nights. Even if darkness was perfect for smuggling it was not good for the soul. And the sort of work he would be doing with the Englishman would need light. Eidi's head was heavy on his shoulder, her body warm against his, and the wind, high in the ship's rigging, was one of the best sounds you could ever hear, while you were safe in harbour.

They slept, while the storm raged and the Faroe Isles were battered by Arctic winds.

2     There was no time left for self-pity, or mulling over the inconsequence of the life he had made for himself. Now, as Richard Bowman entered the massive administrative building of the oil company for which he worked, he realised with some surprise that he was not apprehensive or nervous. Rather, he felt almost abstracted, as if he were a casual observer with little interest in what was about to take place. He had worried that this stage would have been one of the most awkward, a high hurdle to leap. But, of course, he was committed now. The purpose of his future was the powerful force which dragged him through the pettiness and nonsense of the present. There was no more preparing for rebellion; he had rebelled. The past, the safe, sensible, civilised past, with car, house, regular income and all the niceties it bought, was only important if you needed or wanted it. If you did not respect it, it was useless.

Bowman had little need of his past, only what it had taught him. He had no pride in the structure of his previous life or the society in which he had lived. He recognised that society for the monster it was, for the self-gratifying machine it had become. He could no longer sit in a pub and talk about apartheid or 'rights', or hammer a squash ball for two hours a week so that he could call himself fit, or play the businessman with shares in the portfolio . . . There was only one thing that really hurt, and he knew the hurt would last a long time. That was the way the country was now. It was like the song, *Selling England by the Pound*, except that the English way of life was all sold, and no one had noticed or cared any more; and yet, he knew, it was the very last thing that should have been sold. The hypocrisy was the ugliest part. People would send donations and everyone would have an opinion; but the world would be poisoned anyway. The whales would be killed, the trees cut down, and black kids would starve. People would give money but they would not sell their houses to stop the ravaging. They would write to their MPs, but they would not put the bastards up against the wall for not doing their job properly.

The lift hissed to a gentle halt. Bowman caught himself marvelling at the dampers, the wonderful pneumatic springs. We could perfect such things and yet . . . He walked across the luxuriously carpeted lounge towards the reception desk. Even the air-conditioning would not soften his resolve; none of the trappings of his past or present could possibly affect his decisions. He was furious, but not bitter, and certainly not afraid of throwing away the softening aspects of life. A new man was emerging from the shell of Richard Bowman, and this time the world and he had a better understanding. He knew what he owed and what he would have to pay. He was no better than anyone, or anything, else; but he was not any worse either, unless he made the old mistakes.

'I have an appointment,' he told the secretary.

'Yes, sir, Mr Hopkins is expecting you. Please knock and go right in.' He entered the office without knocking; a little thing, but this had to be on his own terms.

The office smelt of power, that strange aura of immunity that a rich organisation possesses. Every company man was answerable to such an office. One's mistakes ended up on bits of print-out on a desk as sterile as the one he stood before. And the man who sat behind it, motioning Bowman to be seated, could have been any one of the thousands of men who hold people's careers, even lives, in their grasp. Behind the executive, Bowman could see the river through the smoked-glass window. It was all so still and quiet. The water shimmered in the weak March sunlight. Hopkins was in silhouette, a menacing touch to intimidate slightly those who had been noticed enough to be drawn to his attention and summoned. There was a moment of

16

silence while they examined one another. Hopkins smiled, though his eyes had not smiled for many years. Bowman looked beyond him again, at the river. Even at that distance it looked so much more vital than the office's anonymity . . . Water, and the sun, wind and sky; even the crowding city could not dull the image. Bowman's new life would be out there. Hopkins was no more than an unpleasant delay, a brief clinging of the old order.

'It seems you wish to leave us,' said the silhouette.

'I *am* leaving, it's as simple as that.' Bowman refused to volunteer anything. Hopkins meant nothing to him; just part of the old existence that he despised, part of what he wished to destroy. The executive would have to ask for anything he wished to know. That would make a change for him, put him at a disadvantage, unnerve him. Hopkins shuffled through the print-out, not really reading it. He knew that he did not hold the dominant position, even there in his own territory.

'We would like to know your reasons. Neither the head of your section nor I have been asked for a reference: it seems you are not seeking a new position.' There lay the kink in the system's smooth running. 'Is this correct?'

'Yes, I am not looking for another job.' The beautiful river appeared to be motionless, but Bowman was strangely aware of the fact that the water he had seen when he had entered the office was already a quarter of a mile downstream, nearer the sea, like the wasted years . . .

'Well, you cannot be retiring, at 34, even on the salary you have commanded here. I trust you do not feel you have been under-valued?' That would have been a joke if it hadn't been so tasteless. Twenty-five thousand a year for drifting around in a submarine in the North Sea, and adapting prototypes for use on the rigs. It was nothing that any engineer could not manage, so long as he did not suffer from claustrophobia and had learnt a little about water. Twenty-five thousand for something which was hardly even dangerous with the modern safety regulations, while the poor sods in the trawlers would struggle for a third of that – in seas where no one ever dared take the submarines. It was ridiculous, Bowman thought; someone was being robbed so that he could earn that much. The oil paid for it? Someone had to pay for the oil. Worst of all, something the silhouette would never understand, the planet was paying for it. And it could not afford that sort of take.

'The pay's fine.' It would have been pointless telling him it was too much, far too much. 'I just don't believe in . . .' But then he realised that explaining would achieve nothing. 'I have no satisfaction in my work with the company.'

'So what are you planning to do now?' Hopkins did not really care. He had simply been offended that someone way below him in the company could treat him with such undisguised contempt. Bowman was not obeying the normal rules. He was bypassing them, ignoring them. It was necessary to understand how it was possible for someone to escape the net. 'I do hope you have not been poached by a competitor.' Of course, that was what he suspected. It was the obvious, safe answer to an annoying human riddle. Bowman was an inconsistency, a speck of dirt on the company's hands. He would have to be washed away with some clean answers.

'I am not going to work for anyone else, just myself.'

'You are taking a lot of training and expertise with you . . .' Now the virtuous attitude, Bowman thought; Hopkins the moralist. And what could he possibly know about the expertise and training? No one trained you to drop 300 feet into black water. You trained yourself. If you could master the fear and obey the instructions that the monitors and dials gave out then you could do it. Anyway, you only did a few dives a month. The rest of the time was spent with electronics and stress diagrams, or playing around in tanks.

'You are not worried about that, and please don't tell me you can't find a replacement. Surely you've already got one. We both know that you have the choice of hundreds in this country alone; and God knows how many Japanese.' Bowman was stifling his rising temper. 'There is nothing we have to say to one another. I am simply leaving the company, honourably, within the terms of my contract. I am not invaluable, any more than you are.' Bowman half-regretted the personal insult.

18

Perhaps it was unnecessary. Hopkins turned in his seat, so that he was in profile against the glowing waters far away. He obscured the vision of his interviewee. He was malevolence on the face of beauty. 'Will that be all?' asked Bowman.

'I believe you are making a serious mistake. Your career is young. For the last year or two it has been noticed that you suffer from a certain lack of conformity. You do realise, of course, that it will be difficult for me, or anyone in this company, to yield good references for you, *when* they are needed.' The embittered voice cut the air, obscuring the distant hum of London traffic.

'I have not asked for references, as you said earlier, and I have no intention of doing so.' The old world was crumbling ineffectually as he retreated from it, while the river slid on, drawing him towards the new life. He stood up.

'None the less,' Hopkins persisted, 'you are taking an important specialisation and industrial knowledge with you and you must realise the restriction that imposes on your freedom. I shall have your case examined.' He swung back in his chair to face Bowman. Their stares met and Bowman could see something vicious in Hopkin's expression. It was the 'industrial knowledge' that was the point. The man had not been brave enough to use the term 'industrial espionage', but he had implied his suspicions. He was the sort of low-principled creature that thrived like a symbiotic organism in the commercial world. Bowman stooped towards the executive, gripped the corners of the desk until his knuckles whitened.

'However I choose to use my knowledge is entirely up to me.' The words came out harsh in the still atmosphere. 'I will not be selling any of your precious secrets, either abroad or at home. And there is no "case", as you put it.' He dismissed himself, pushed abruptly away from the desk and left the seething Hopkins in his chair. Leaving the office he felt an immediate necessity to escape the sterility of the place, find a bridge over the river, or a quiet length of bank, where he could watch and think. He hurried out of the building, suddenly cold in the early spring air. A dry wind battled around the tower blocks, wafting

19

hamburger cartons and sweet wrappers against the legs of passers-by. He walked north, towards the river, towards the future.

Crossing Waterloo Bridge, Bowman took the steps down to the Embankment. He felt quite peaceful there on the wide pavement, the cars speeding past the trees, the brown waters of the Thames billowing twenty feet below, the stark sun and the cold. There in the middle of London he felt a freedom he had not known for too long. He walked slowly upstream towards Hungerford Bridge where he decided on the spur of the moment to take a trip on an early-season pleasure cruiser. He paid his fare and sat on one of the deserted deck seats in the bow.

The boat slipped downstream, beneath the bridges, close to the grey wall of HMS *Belfast* and on towards Greenwich. Bowman was warm with his thoughts. No one could interfere now. The venture had begun. He had taken the first steps, tiny and yet positive, and he had escaped the womb of previous experience. What lay beyond, still in imagination and tenuous plans, was thrilling: frightening also, but full of purpose, reason for his new life to exist. What was it Cervantes wrote of Don Quixote: something about being faithful to the cause? That was the most important thing, to have your cause and allow not a fraction of your soul to stray. While you had that no one could touch you.

He wondered about the two men on board *Hannah*. Where would they be now? Having their own problems with the Authorities, or running from big seas. Perhaps they would be delivering another illegal load, or standing off-shore, waiting for darkness. He was certain of one thing; that Claus and Jens would be waiting for him, for the communication via Esbjerg. And it would not be long now – under two months – even though there was still much to be accomplished before then.

The river widened, and the pleasure boat turned to retrace its passage towards central London. Bowman mentally gathered himself together for the next steps into his venture.

Directive to: *Home Office, Department of National Security*.


Ref. SW Industrial 3320

Investigation recommendation, code 3, subject: *Bowman, Richard Raef.*

British, age 34.
B.Sc.(Electrical Eng.) M.Sc.(Materials Eng.) Ph.D.(Marine Engineering) (King's College, London).

Formerly submariner, North Fire oil company.

*Details*: Left high-salaried job, promising career, with no apparent new employment. Special knowledge in miniature submarines. Previous access to Official Secrets, level 2, and company restricted information on submarine design.

Suspicion of industrial espionage, or possible foreign power 'head hunt' in order to obtain specialist skills and restricted information. Situation alerted by North Fire Executive.


*Investigation authorised for MI5, section C,* middle priority.

# 3

Emeritus Professor Partridge welcomed Richard Bowman into his laboratory with his characteristic, flamboyant friendliness. 'It's been so long!' he cried. 'Come in, come in. It's *so* good to see you. Tell me the news; I've been hearing whispers, you've been a naughty fellow . . .' He hauled Bowman by the arm into the confused sanctity of his lab. 'You can't keep secrets from old Partridge you know, not so long as you're a water engineer.' He had not changed. His few strands of white hair still flew about as he twitched his head from side to side. The fluorescent lamps shone on his wrinkled scalp as it writhed over the wide skull. And his blue eyes made you laugh as they winked and saw through you and seemed to belong to the being who had invented mischievousness. As he dragged Bowman to a stool a circuit board fell out of a tattered pocket of his lab-coat. He kicked it under one of the numerous work benches. 'Couldn't get the thing to work anyway. Jameson's fault; can't solder properly. Have to do it all myself if I want it to work. Oh Dicky, I miss not having you around. Mind you, you were just as useless as any of these young idiots they send to me for a training. Well, come on, speak up, has the cat got it, or what?'

'Prof, you silly old fool, no one can ever get a word in when you're around. Just shut up and listen. I've flogged the house, left my job, said goodbye to Vicky and I need a bloody big favour.'

'Vicky – you've said goodbye? Oh dear, I thought you two would get married or something.' That was just like him, thought Bowman. Never mind the job or the house; straight to the important facts. 'Had a row did you? Can't make amends? Poor girl. Your fault of course. Always told her she was far too good for you. I advised her to find a younger version of me, someone who would really appreciate her. See to that kettle, there's a good chap, we'll have a cuppa and sort it all out. Oh my goodness, will you look at that!' He pointed at a strange piece of machinery. 'They can't even put a simple dial in straight nowadays. Look at it! They think it doesn't matter, but it does, it does. How could anybody be expected to read that properly. Damned Nips wouldn't do that. I keep telling them, if they want to compete with the East then their product has to be the best, the *very best*. Otherwise they just needn't bother. Oh dear, dear. Are you in some sort of trouble, old chap?'

'No, not yet, but I probably will be. At the moment I'm just not very popular with my old firm, that's all.'

'Why, what are you up to? Why did you leave? Kettle's boiling, two sugars.'

'Something to do with job satisfaction, Prof, or life dis-satisfaction. There's something I have to do.'

'Oh, yes, yes of course.' The professor waved his arms about and slapped his thighs, as if he had worked it all out. 'Visions, is it? Got a cause have we? Yes, you're the type. Naïve, stupid, head-strong, must make a mark. Ha, but you're past thirty aren't you? Bit old for saving the world and flirting with history.' His eyes flashed, but he moved a hand on to the young man's shoulder. 'What are you up to, Richard?'

'I'm not going to save the world, but I'm going to have a go at putting right a little bit of my own. That's why I've come to you. I can't tell you exactly what I'm going to do; but I am asking you to help me all the same.'

'Ah, so you don't think I'm useless then. Everyone around here thinks I'm scatty you know. That's why they made me Emeritus: it's a polite way of saying I'm past it. Are you going to pour that tea before it gets cold? Bet it's like the tasteless dishwater you always used to brew. While you do that you can tell me what you want.' He sat himself down and lit his pipe. It appeared to be the same one he had had all those years ago, more chewed than smoked.

'I want a shallow-water sonar device with variable range, active and passive. It must be multi-directional. Most of all it should feed its analysed signals to a monitor screen and accept commands from a keyboard – I will give you the syntax. It will work on the lowest electrical currents possible. I can step the voltage up or down, but my main-line is twelve volts – direct.' The professor looked at his old student for a moment, then roared with laughter.

'*Small* problem! Well, Dicky, thank you *very* much. You're not going to tell me what you're up to, but you want me to build a machine like that. Sounds fishy, you scallywag. Is it illegal? No, don't tell me; of course it is. Oh no, quite impossible, out of the question.' He took a sip of tea and frowned. 'Long range is the problem, you know, especially in shallow water: too much background. Have to emit all sorts of frequencies and analyse the echo. Horrid; bound to be unreliable. Worst bit's the programming; lots of loops and "gosubs". Uses up stacks of memory time. Would take me six months to work out the software, never mind the machine. No, impossible, I can't do it.'

'When can you let me have it, Prof? You have a month at the most.'

Partridge sighed. 'Dicky, just tell me that you are *sure* whatever you are up to is right. It must be pretty important for you to give up everything like that, especially Vicky. But I don't want to see either of you unhappy. You gave me some of the best times of my career when you worked in this lab.' His stare was intense and sincere. 'One can't possibly be happy if what is being done is wrong.'

'Prof, I swear to you that I never believed in anything so much as this. It *is* important and it *is* right.'

'Fair enough, you young fool, so give me some details about this wretched device. Is it to be attached to something stationary or mobile? Will it . . .'

24

And so Bowman involved his old friend in the first event of his new life. It was odd, when he thought of it. So little of his former existence had survived intact. His clothes, moods, even his inner thoughts seemed to belong to a man he was only beginning to know. But the Professor had come through, with him, into the present. Partridge was timeless. He belonged to all eras. He was solid. Bowman believed in the Professor even though, beyond the realm of the plans for his own future, he believed in little that was comforting.

When he left the Professor, typing away on a console and scribbling on bits of paper, it was dark outside. A cold wind rushed through the city and all the lights of offices, cars and buses whirled around him as he hurried along the pavement. His thoughts were spinning with relief and excitement. Now, with the Professor on his side, the plan was viable. Soon he could say goodbye to London and move on to the next phase with the knowledge that he was to have one of the essential components, and at least the understanding of a man he loved and respected.

Now he had to collect together the materials for the rest of the machinery. He had managed at last to complete the conveyancing for the cottage in Scotland, by the loch, and he hoped to be completing the sale of his North London home within a week. That would provide the money he needed, and the remote cottage would afford the necessary privacy.

It began to rain and Bowman pulled up his collar. It was good, he thought, to be one's own master and to be in a position to do exactly what you thought was right. That was freedom, as close as any man could come to it, so long as the inner man was at peace; and that only came from obeying your conscience. He walked along Kingsway towards Holborn, immune to the bustling crowds, the rushing traffic and the driving rain.

4  Up on the great Faroes banks at last, the pilot whale school shouldered the pressing seas. Four hundred whales swam northward, west of Suduroy, the most southern island in the Faroes group. The leader pulsed out a continuous rhythmic sonar, guiding the followers. The water tumbled in a confusion of upwelling and tidal currents, now spinning, vortexing, then thrown in an explosion of spray at the sky. Deeper, on the warmest layers of the ever-weakening North Atlantic Drift, were the squid, pulsing and water-jetting their passage into the high latitudes of the ocean, now that spring, and lengthening days, had arrived.

The whales were following this food source, and the light, from the deep seas of the Faroes-Shetland gap. Here, on the banks, they would feed and breed, and pause until they were ready for the big run towards the deeps off southern Iceland, and vast shoals of summer squid. But it was still early spring and they laboured in the heaving groundswell.

Their backs rolled at the surface and the crack and spume of their blows spat into the wind, like a hundred gun-shots as a hundred shadows turned on the grey sea, and another hundred, and again, bothering the already troubled waves.

The leader whale sang his unfailing song, which penetrated the noisy seas for more than a mile in any direction, so that the little ones would not be lost if they dived for squid and fell behind the main school. None had been lost, even during the long journey across the gap from Shetland during equinoctial storms. Their sonar bound them, the massive domes of their heads transmitting their perpetual chatter, while always re-

26

ceiving the leader's signal. When he turned east, four hundred whales turned east, ramming into a surge of currents.

They rounded the headland beneath Rakkur cliffs and pushed into Suduroy Sound where the squid shoals were dense. A fluid curve of animal motion spilled into the deep. A new note swept the sea, a crackling rhythmic pulse as the whales sought their prey, and fuzzy echoes which only they could understand, then the thumping, bang, bang, as they hit the squid far down in the dark water.

Surfacing again, the whales rested, protected from the full force of the wind by Suduroy's mountains. They wallowed, their voices falling quiet, only the leader's growling sonar giving them unity among the chaotic chuck of waves. The young ones pressed close in by the flanks of the big females and sought protection from the ceaseless turbulence. The only whales that had not fed were the very old or the very sick. These would leave the school while still in Faroese waters. They would detach themselves from the sonar web, the framework of the school, and they would die.

The storms were protecting the pilot whales by hiding them among steep seas and rain-filled air. The vapour of their blows was as nothing against the continuous shocks and streaks of white foam, the crash of spray. The sounds of their blows, close inshore, were swamped by the tumble and hiss of waves on rock. No human eyes saw the whales and the school was safe, its presence unsuspected.

Soon, when the north winds fell, the rain ceased and the thick mists cleared, there would be no safety in these waters. The whales' stark black forms would be clearly visible against the sea's opalescent blue, their blows as obvious as clouds in the otherwise empty skies. The watchers would not miss them.

# 5

Richard Bowman woke suddenly from a troubled sleep. He rubbed his eyes, disabusing himself of the violent images which had filled his mind as he had slept. Then more rational thoughts crowded in and he lay there examining each one. Always, however, there was a single image, a memory, that stood clear and overshadowed all others. It confronted him. He saw the beautiful islands in the cobalt sea; the sunshot, pure waters and the Nordic longboats with their brilliant paintwork that glistened under the glaring northern sun. Then the scene was a confused antithesis of the idyllic backdrop. Bowman tried to think about something else; but nothing was strong enough to dispel the recollection. The sea bulged as whale-backs rose and the boats closed in while spears and harpoons, hooks and knives drove into the dark shapes; and the screams were amplified as each blade cut, as the tide ran red.

It was not the killing that haunted him. Bowman had long ago acknowledged that. It was the suffering, the way it happened. And those memories had plagued him for almost ten years, and they had become more vivid over the intervening time, even though he knew they had not become exaggerated. Such total brutality and cruelty could not be increased. It was already on the limit.

He sat in bed with the light on, rubbing his temples as he calmed down. It was just before midnight when he heard the key in the lock and the slight creak as the front door opened. He rushed out of bed, down the stairs and into the hall. His shoulders sagged and he relaxed as he saw the woman.

'You look awful,' she said as he stood before her. She brushed past him and walked into the kitchen.

'I was asleep. Vicky, what are you doing here?'

'You were dreaming again. Come on, I know that look. Was it your islands?' He nodded, but he was not thinking about the nightmares or memories any more.

'This will only make things more difficult. We had agreed not to see each other until this business is all over.'

'That was last week. Anyway, more difficult for whom? For you maybe, with your mysterious quest.' She smiled sarcastically and yet he could see something more in her expression. Inevitably it was not so easy for her. She would not be the one taking part in the venture. Hers would not be the physical actions and involvement which would make their separation bearable for him. Indeed, she would know nothing of the course of events. She would wait, and endure the unknown. She saw a defensiveness come across his expression. 'It's not that I don't believe in the value of what you're planning. It's just the . . .' Desperately, it seemed, she tried to express how she felt without putting an even greater strain on their relationship '. . . futility and destruction; I just *know* that you will destroy more than you will protect, or save.'

'Vicky, we've been over it all before, a dozen times.' She sat at the kitchen table, watching him, inquisitive, perplexed. Her coat was still unbuttoned, her scarf around her neck. She looked as if she too had not slept well.

'And we can't move beyond this stalemate, because you refuse to see my point. Darling,' she implored, 'I know you are working through all the technical problems. You can master those; but they're easy, don't you see that? It's the human problems, the weaknesses we all have, all those things you can't possibly foresee. They'll creep up on you no matter how beautifully and safely you prepare . . .'

'You're over-reacting, Vicky.'

'Am I? So why have those nightmares come back? Why do you look ten years older than you really are? And why the hell

29

do you need . . . ?' Suddenly she looked guiltily down at her hands on the table.

'You've been talking to Prof.'

Defiantly again she turned to face him. 'Prof. phoned me. He's as worried about you as I am. God knows why, but he thinks the world of you and doesn't want to see you wasted.'

'Actually it's you he's trying to protect. You're like a daughter to him.'

'He knows what you're going to put his sonar device into.'

'Of course he does; but he doesn't know what I'm going to use it for.' She shook her head, resigned to his stubbornness, the impossibility of changing the situation. His memories of the islands and the great whales were stifling and there was a fog in his mind, like a veil of bloody spray thrashed into the air.

'Do you want me to leave?'

'You *should* leave; but no, not now; tomorrow.' He held out his hand to her. She shook her head and sighed. Together they walked upstairs. For a brief moment during the dawn of Richard Bowman's venture, the islands in his memory lay in a calm, untroubled sea where there were no whales and no harpoons.


Surveying the room, later that night, in the orange sodium-glow from the street lights, he saw her clothes spread haphazardly around the floor. The dishevelled bedclothes draped loosely across the lower half of her body while her dark hair sprawled over the pillows, untidy, unruly, yet, to him, as wildly erotic as her sprawled limbs and her breasts, firmed by her upraised and outstretched arms. She slept, her eyebrows and lashes appearing to be etched, strangely, on her pale face in the faint light. There was no trace of her anxiety as she slept, no frown to spoil her lovely features. Almost, she was as she had been all those years earlier, when he had first met her; but that, he knew, was a deception produced by the light and her sleep. Later he would see her as the woman she had become, the slight but definite wrinkles of her thirty-three years adding their character to her face.

He thought about the years they had had together, recalling the sensuous turbulence of the beginning as they passed through student life, when responsibilities belonged to other people, when energy was boundless, and how they had longed to share that energy, to fuse it. He remembered walking with her, hand in hand, down Charing Cross Road to Embankment Station, standing in the Underground train, almost shaking with excitement as their taut bodies brushed and bumped together with the carriage's motion. Then the short winter afternoons in her room, the peculiar emotional pain as they pushed their bodies apart and picked up the discarded books from the floor and forced one another to learn something of their chosen disciplines. Everywhere there were always books; law and logic, Kant's philosophy folded around Einsteinian mechanics, her *From College to Articles* and his *Theory of the Quantised Universe*. They had found it all so important at the time, life so earnest, exams so final, bodies so firm and strong and vital.

Later, as careers developed, they began to see the limits of their energy. Horizons, hitherto unimagined, bound them, still a long way away, but there all the same and threatening to close in upon them. They simply lost the abandon of youth. Their work, more than anything else, separated them. She, destined for the Bar, had her sights on the law courts, while he became fascinated by sophisticated machinery that could be used in hostile environments. The North Sea and submarines; it had been a good learning ground, but within the bounds of unions and the oil company, and limited scope, the job had become too pedantic. There was little future – the oil would soon be gone – and no *vision*.

And through those times they had seen less of each other and more of other people; but their understanding for one another had not weakened. They were as one body, becoming more differentiated. Even as they loved others they could not love one another less.

Vicky stirred and opened her eyes, immediately looking straight at him in the room's dim light. 'You ought to sleep. An adventure needs a clear head to form it.'

'It is already formed. I don't think I could stop it now even if I tried. Besides, I'm not tired. I've been asleep for years, and only just woken up.'

'Don't talk about such nonsense. Come and keep me warm.'

### Home Office MI5 – Section C

Ref. SW Industrial 3321

Preliminary investigation Bowman, Richard. No links found with foreign power agents. No links found national or international companies.
Private London house sold. Cottage bought North-west Scotland, isolated location. Recent contact with old professor at King's College: Emeritus Professor D. C. Partridge, FRS. Recent purchase of glass-fibre and electronic materials from sources linked with company North Fire. No illegal materials.

Recent Social: Girlfriend; Chambers, Victoria (Company lawyer, Elswick, Elswick and Boyd). Two dinner parties with non-suspicious and non-listed persons.

Recent business: None apparent.

*File suspended awaiting further directives.*

Willoughby, Assistant Head of Section C, frowned as he finished reading the investigation summary. He glanced back at the original directive. He was annoyed, wondering why they always sent the middle priority investigations to him. They rarely turned out to be important, and when they did they were stolen by Royce, Head of Section. There was nothing here. The oil company was upset at losing a key employee, that was all. Bowman was obviously 'opting out' for a peaceful life, hence the isolated cottage. The meeting with the professor was a social call; his old teacher. It all added up to that; a loser who could

32

not take the pressure. But there were the strange purchases. They did not fit into the image of someone who was opting out.

Willoughby did not like things which did not fit perfectly into place. There always had to be an underlying structure of rationale beneath intelligence operations and investigations; but, surely this one was neat enough. He paused as he moved the bits of paper towards the suspended files, then changed his mind. What the harm, he would give it another week, it was not his money. He stamped the investigation summary *Middle Priority* and wrote: 'continue for one week and report'.

# 6

North-western Scotland that March was cold. Everything looked scrubbed clean; especially so after the dust and damp and grime of London. Bowman stood on the loch shore and closed his eyes, revelling in the twin pleasures of the sun's slight warmth on his face and the crispness of the air. A wind from the north chopped the water into an uneasy wave, while the heather, in which he stood, was bare, combed by winter. The three thousand foot peak to the south, Ben Farewell, was starkly etched against the sky. He was surrounded by an ancient, awesome land. The cold, he supposed, had protected it from change, and also its remoteness from flat, fertile land. The hurricane winds of each equinox and the high rainfall also kept the place free of human development, discouraging those travellers of long ago from settling. There was, however, one house on the shores of Loch Farewell, a small croft that had not been occupied for twenty-five years. Bowman had bought it.

The only approach to Farewell Lodge was across the loch itself. A rough track had cut away from the coast road which traverses, haphazardly, the north of Sutherland. Bowman had driven the Land Rover for three miles along the track which led down to the loch's eastern shore, winding through a mixed terrain of alluvial meadows, rocky screes tumbling towards the loch, and birch woods, spindly and gnarled after centuries of being left alone to colonise the crags of gneiss and granite. He found the estate boat, which he had taken over on purchase of the croft, pulled up on a tiny gravel beach beneath a spinney of birch and rowan. Directly across the loch, which was half a mile wide at this point, lay his new home.

The boat was wooden and heavy, very difficult for one man to manoeuvre on land, but it was fairly large. It would be more than just a lifeline at the Lodge, it would also have to carry all the materials and machinery. Now it was about to make its first journey under his ownership, carrying, as well as himself, a heavy supply of food, cement, a diesel powered generator, timber and two heavily-packed suitcases. He wondered, briefly, how many dozens of trips it would make over the next two months. It had already served fly-fishers and shepherds through the past twenty or thirty stormy years.

He launched the boat into the loch's sparkling waters, started the Seagull outboard and steered towards the Lodge. The landscape encircled him, the lonely vista of hills streaked with lines of heather and the torrents of burns in spate with melt-water, the tall mountain four miles to the south, and the open Atlantic, beyond the short river, three miles to the north. His skin tingled with a weird, excited sensation. He was like those who took refuge in the desert sands, or the mountain-men who shunned an easier life on the lowlands. He wished he could have trapped that moment, and the following few days, for eternity. But even in the wish he realised that he would then merely be an escapee, a hostage to his own weaknesses. There, at Farewell, he could know a freedom from mankind; but with his venture he could have a freedom *among* mankind.

The Lodge was in a poor state of repair. Bats and owls had roosted in the two bedrooms, while sheep had made free with downstairs. There was little more than superficial damage, however, for the building was a simple but sturdy construction of stone and hard-woods beneath a slate roof. Brick and tile would long since have tumbled beneath the fierce winds, but the three-foot thick stone walls had withstood seasonal batter-ing, and the estate owners had recently repaired the roof in order to make the place saleable. They had bargained on finding a man like Bowman; apparently a refugee from society who did not mind much about rain and isolation. They could not possibly know why he was running, or what he was running towards, and for what reason he needed the isolation. So far as they were concerned, and he had taken pains not to disillusion them, he was an artist, with hermit tendencies. His privacy was thus assured, aided by the local geography.

There were other reasons, besides its immunity from observation, why he had chosen this place. He had to be close to the sea – for when the time came – and he needed easy access to a deep, fresh-water loch. Farewell was ideal, even more so due to the fact that he had both found and bought it so easily. He had first seen the little building ten years earlier while on a sea-trout fishing tour of northern Scotland. Since then he had returned several times to fish for the loch's legendary trout. Each time he had gone over to the Lodge for a visit and had wondered at its strange beauty. Quite by chance he had heard that the owners of the massive estate on which it stood were in financial trouble as a result of the death of the old laird. A few telephone calls and ten thousand pounds had secured for him the Lodge and surrounding five acres together with access across the loch.

For the next week he did live the existence of a hermit. He spent his time cleaning and repairing the dirt and damage of all the years the Lodge had been unoccupied. Downstairs there was just the one large room, incorporating a living area and a kitchen, which consisted of a fireplace on a raised hearth, an enamel sink with no taps, upturned boxes and planks which formed a table and some more planks bracketed to the walls as shelves. Against the south wall stood a larger fireplace above which an old oak beam traversed at a tilt and in which were engraved the initials of a previous occupier, '*MM*', and the carefully carved words, '*farewell my home*'. Bowman often tried to work out whether the inscriber was referring to Farewell Lodge as being his home, or if he was simply saying goodbye. He believed, intuitively, that it was the latter.

There was no plasterwork in the Lodge, other than between the oak and birch joists in the ceilings, the walls being mortared, inside and out, between the stones and then whitewashed. The windows, three downstairs facing south and east and one in each bedroom, were tiny, the thick glass being set into surprisingly sound hard-wood frames. Once he had cleaned everything and repaired what he could, the atmosphere was of charm and peace, and solidity against an inclement environment; though it was then, and always would be, a frontierman's or pioneer's home, a refuge for a wanderer who sought only four walls, shelter from the sky and warmth, among the wilderness.

He had but one brief visitor, of the human kind, during that first week. A shepherd, passing by on the hill to the west, saw him laying a pipe from the burn, which ran close to the north wall, towards the kitchen.

'Ye dinnae plan tae live here?' The man leaned against a sheep staff.

'I certainly plan to, yes; at least in the summer,' Bowman shouted in reply. The shepherd shook his head but he was smiling pleasantly.

'Only an Englishman would want tae, I suppose. Are ye a fisher?' Bowman replied that he was. 'Aye, that might explain it.' Then he waved and shambled off after his dogs.

The intruder, however, had given a warning. Bowman could not guarantee that he, or his companion when he arrived, could work totally unobserved. It probably did not matter whether or not a shepherd saw the hardware; but all men talk. It was possible that word of mouth would spread some information of strange goings-on by Loch Farewell.

He kept both fires going whenever he was awake. Fuel was no problem, for behind the Lodge, reaching along the banks of the burn away up the hill was thick deciduous woodland, littered with fallen trunks and branches. For a couple of hours each day he gathered wood and dragged it to the pile which was ever-growing despite the consumption. The fires cheered the place, especially at night when the sounds from outside of wind, curlews and foxes were the sounds of loneliness. Sometimes, during the grey dawn, a Peregrine falcon would screech from her hunting post, an old stump at the wood's edge. Her piercing call would seem to awaken the loch-side, yet still all living creatures with fear.

As the falcon flew to gain height for her lethal stoop,

disappearing among the dark scuds and storm-clouds hurrying across the sky from the west, Bowman would get up and prepare for the day. His first job always consisted of starting the generator and heating some water on the newly-lit fires . . . So the falcon and he would both go about their precarious life-styles. She was the huntress; and he too, soon, was to be a sort of hunter, with all the stealth and cunning of that great killer-bird.

He found, however, as the days passed, that he was thinking less of plans for the future. He slept well, without the nightmares, for he was working physically and extremely hard. His mind was occupied with the intricacies of making the Lodge into a comfortable habitation, while he toiled to accommodate his enthusiasm. There came a day, however, when he realised the household chores were over, when no more could be done without a large injection of building materials, and, besides, it was the end of March. His companion in the venture, beside the Danes, was to arrive on April 3rd.

Attached to the south-western wall of the Lodge was a large outbuilding which he considered perfect for their work. He had cleared out the debris it had gathered during its past function as store-house for the junk of several generations of crofters, and the mess caused by more recent habitation by birds and various mammals. Hanging from the rafters was a tarnished brass oil-lamp. He polished it until it shone and placed it in one of the downstairs windows where the erstwhile crofters had lit it, to guide their homecoming boat across the loch at night.

Those last two days alone were to be busy in different ways. He had to travel to Inverness, perhaps even as far as Glasgow or Edinburgh, to collect more provisions, and materials that he had overlooked while back in London. This was also to be his last chance to recall and examine the details of the plans before his companions became irrevocably involved. In Inverness, also, he had arranged a meeting with the founder member of *World-Watch*, the most assertive of all conservation groups with, it was rumoured, close allegiance with authoritative MPs on the Left of the House. The press referred to the group as an 'ecological alliance'.

On climbing into the Land Rover, Bowman glanced back over the loch's pitching waters, sad that he was leaving and knowing that on his return events would have become more complicated. He wished he could have frozen the little idyll over there on Farewell's west shore, thrown it back to some previous epoch to protect it from the future. It had given him a sense of peace; but he needed anger, and not to run from the mainstream of what seemed evil in life; but rather to confront it head-on. Therein, he believed, might not lie happiness, but certainly self-respect, which was the next best thing.

### Home Office MI5 – Section C

Ref. SW Industrial 3322

Continued investigation; Bowman, Richard. No links with *known* foreign power agents. Two telephone conversations (untapped on middle priority) abroad. Number traced in both cases to Portland, Oregon, USA. Receiver; Fitzgerald, George Albert; known front-line conservationist and anti-Reaganist.

Recent Social/Business: Bowman has arranged a meeting in Inverness with Heath-Morton, Oliver, Founder member of *World-Watch*, a conservation group with strong Left-Wing membership. Heath-Morton considered a subversive by Section B and is monitored continuously. Bowman's telephone conversation has been taped (tape archive SL 3322/ 7866): no definitive information other than meeting place and time at hotel in Inverness.

*File remaining open on middle priority awaiting further directives.*

Willoughby smiled with self-satisfaction and lit a congratulatory cigarette. With a flourish he stamped the renewal section *High Priority* and wrote: 'Open full investigative file and telephone monitor'. It was strange, he thought, that a week ago he had thought that Bowman was a drop-out, a danger to nobody. Now the man was linked with two listed men; a foreign subversive and the head of a British conservation group. Bowman was off the industrial espionage list and had become a conservationist, which was another word for subversive, or even, when the national feeling was intense enough, a terrorist. And he was Willoughby's.

# 7

'Mr Heath-Morton sends his apologies, Sir, and asked us to pass this on to you,' said the receptionist at Oliver Heath-Morton's hotel. Bowman opened the envelope and read the message inside:

Sorry about the secrecy, but, as you will learn, it is necessary. It is for your own good as much as mine. Will explain all when I see you. I will be at the café in Ness Street until 2 p.m. It might be better if you take some care to avoid being followed. Oliver H-M.

Bowman screwed up the note. With some alarm he pondered the implications of what Heath-Morton had written. *World-Watch* was noted as being not extreme, concentrating rather on peaceful and influential activity. Its members were not cranks and the founder of such an organisation, surely, would not be paranoid. When Bowman had spoken to him over the telephone he had sounded sincere and intelligent. He must have had good reason to write what he had.

It was half-past twelve in the afternoon. He asked the receptionist where he would find Ness Street. He left the hotel and walked through a fine, warm drizzle. At first he made no pains to disguise his direction. He could not believe that anyone would wish to follow him. There was no reason for it. Then the words of Heath-Morton's note came back to him – 'It might be better . . .' He glanced behind him, taking in a normal scene in Inverness on a wet spring day. Two women hurried along together on the far side of the road. Walking in the same direction as Bowman were two men, the first, about to overtake him, he guessed from his clothes was a railway employee or possibly a dock worker. The second, fifty yards behind, was a well-dressed man who seemed to be in no particular hurry . . . Bowman turned left at a crossroads and then left again, now travelling away from Ness Street. He walked quickly and did not look behind him. He turned into a dingy little road and entered a newsagent's. He took his time about buying a newspaper and pretended to be looking at some paperbacks. From his position in the shop he could see into the street. He was watching as the man he had seen behind him, near the hotel, walked slowly past. The man's clothing was somehow far too 'rural-gentleman' for a rainy shopping day in Inverness. He wore a new thornproof jacket, unzipped, over a beautiful tweed jacket. The neck of an expensive jumper exposed a shirt collar and tie. His trousers were casual but neatly pressed and his shoes had not been bought off the shelf of a chain-store. He half-turned to look into the shop. For the briefest of moments the men stared at one another.

There had to be an explanation, some perfectly ordinary reason. Bowman stifled the urge to confront the stranger. Oliver Heath-Morton would explain. He was the one, after all, who had given the warning.

He decided to run. There was no way that Thornproof could then stay with him through the streets of Inverness, without making it obvious. To anyone who noticed, Bowman was just hurrying to avoid the rain, anyone, that is, except Thornproof. He knew that Bowman knew . . .

Bowman ran along the river bank, crossed by the main road-bridge and weaved his way around the shoppers. To catch his breath he sat for a minute or two in the photo-cubicle in Woolworths before recommencing his dash, finally towards his destination. Half way down Ness Street he paused and looked around. Thornproof was nowhere to be seen. Bowman crossed the road and entered the café. It was a little after 1 p.m.

The smoky, dirty café was noisy and full. Abruptly, Bowman realised that he had no idea what Heath-Morton looked like. Besides the woman and two girls behind the counter, everyone was male. There were no suits here, or thornproof jackets, or bright leather shoes. He saw plimsolls and suedes, tough workmen's boots, painters' overalls, oily hands of maintenance men; he smelt the hot greasiness of any such café at lunch time. It was a friendly place. He bought a cup of coffee and sat down with his back to the café window in the only available chair which was at a table for two. The man opposite him glanced jadedly over his newspaper. He smelt of fish. The docks were only a few hundred yards away.

People began to leave the café. Bowman had been there three-quarters of an hour and had seen no one who he thought could be Heath-Morton. He began to wonder if there might be another café in Ness Street. He was about to go and ask at the counter when the man opposite him put down his paper and smiled at him.

'I'm Oliver Heath-Morton. Shall we have another cup of coffee?'

'You! I, I never suspected . . .'

'Good. I like to move around unobserved. Keep your voice down, there's a good chap. As I mentioned in my note, it is necessary to take care.' While Bowman sat perplexed, Heath-Morton went to fetch more coffee. No one could possibly have suspected him of being a founder member of anything other than a fishermen's union. His greying hair was unruly, his face gaunt and lined. His clothes were typical of the trawlermen and Firth fishermen one saw around that part of Inverness. The smell of fish was very strong. His manner was casual. He must have been well practised in the art of deception. He returned to their table with the thick china mugs. 'Well, I think we can talk privately now. Firstly, I must say that I am very sorry about the sinister arrangements. I suspect from your attitude when you came in that you were followed?'

'Yes, I'm sure I was; at first anyway. I ran a mile or two through the streets. I'm certain no one followed me here. I was hoping you would be able to explain.'

'And so I will, I promise, and a few more things besides. May

43

I ask you a few questions first?' In his face, beyond the lines and stubble, Bowman now saw an intelligent man. The features gave the impression, also, as did his voice, of utmost sincerity.

'The last time we spoke on the phone I suggested you kept your plans to yourself and your companions. Have you done that?'

'Yes, obviously the fewer people that know about it the greater are our chances of success.'

'Good, because if certain people hear of your intentions you will be stopped, immediately and finally.'

'Oliver, that sounds ridiculous. It might be a little illegal, but . . .'

'It's much worse than illegal, it's *political*,' interrupted Heath-Morton. 'You will be treading on the toes of governments, or at least offending government policy by exposing sordid details of the system, and a foreign government at that. I tell you, if they even suspect you they will take whatever measures they need in order to silence you permanently.'

'Oh, come on, I can't believe that. Surely you're over-reacting!'

'Am I?' he replied, sitting back in his chair. 'Then you tell me why you were followed.'

'Something to do with you, I suppose. I was followed from *your* hotel.'

'Yes, something to do with me. I am the leader of an influential conservation group which has its questing fingers in a hundred different pies in a dozen countries. I have far more enemies than friends. I am followed wherever I go, my phones are tapped, which is why I always called you from non-traceable sources after our first conversation, and I should think the SIS have as many photographs of me as of any suspected terrorist who passes through Heathrow. To them I am a terrorist, or at least an anarchist, waiting to strike where and when I can. I am a known dissident, hated by our right-wing government. In the event of the threat of war I would be arrested, along with other "subversives", and silenced, one way or another.' Again he paused, his stare testing Bowman for a reaction. 'Please, please do not underestimate what you are playing with; your only chance of success is secrecy. You are taking a great risk at this moment, just by being with me. I only hope you have not been photographed.'

'O.K., one could easily be convinced by all that. You are very persuasive; but, I'm sorry, I simply can't accept that it can be as serious as you say.' Heath-Morton rubbed the stubble on his chin. He seemed tired. Bowman had the impression that the man had been trying for a long time to persuade people of matters he knew he understood better than they did. Even as Bowman spoke his doubts he had the strongest suspicion that Heath-Morton was right and was not exaggerating.

'Greenpeace', Heath-Morton said slowly, 'learned the hard way. They had known for some time that certain governments, including our own, would continually ignore the wishes and needs of ordinary people in order to achieve a short-term objective. But even they were not expecting the French SIS to bomb their boat and commit murder. It happened though, didn't it? And that was not the first time, nor will it be the last. *World-Watch* have documented evidence of dozens of government or secret service activities like the *Rainbow Warrior* incident. Some are rather more distasteful and macabre.'

'Why don't you use that evidence and expose them?'

'We will, but only when the time is right. If we moved now, on anything serious, we would be obliterated; it's as simple as that. When the time comes our journalists, scientists, ministers – all of us – will hit out; but, believe me, the timing has to be perfect. We have not the hardware or financial backing of certain government offices. And, I fear, those offices act with rather less principle than we do, all in the interests of the State and national security, of course.' He laughed cynically. 'Am I putting you off?'

'You're certainly alerting me. You make it sound dangerous.'

'It *is* dangerous, one of the most dangerous activities in the western world. You will be labelled a conservationist. If they catch you taking direct action your label will be no better than that of a terrorist. They will say things of you that would make

45

your mother disown you. Then they'll lock you away. Of course, if they get the chance they will keep it all very quiet and you will simply disappear or suffer an unfortunate accident; but if you make your case publicly, they will destroy you. I swear they have the means and the desire to do it. Furthermore,' he insisted, 'you have very little chance of getting away with this venture of yours, even if the SIS do not become involved.' He looked quizzically at Bowman. 'Well, are you still going to do it?'

'Oh yes, without question. I can't back down now. Could you turn your back on *World-Watch*?'

'Ah, but I am too involved. I am, essentially, *World-Watch*. You could stop now, before you're committed . . .'

'No, no; like you, I am what I believe. Without those beliefs there's nothing. SIS, the law and politics apart; I have to go ahead.'

'Yes, well in that case I will help you as much as I can. You must realise, however, that your activities must not be linked with *World-Watch*. You could damage our credibility enormously if your plans go wrong. I see these years as a time when organisations like ours are consolidating their positions in the political world. To be effective, when it counts, our image has to be whiter than white. Realise also that if necessary I will deny absolutely any links with your activities in order to protect *World-Watch*.'

'I understand. You know, I do not need your support, only some information about the area and what is happening out there. No one seems to know very much about the Faroes and I can hardly go and ask the Danish government or the Admiralty, can I? Your organisation has carried out a scientific investigation of the problem. I would like to see the details of that investigation. Not the report itself that you published in your pamphlet. I want all the "background". It might help.'

'It might indeed.' He opened a battered old carry-all at his side and took out a large brown envelope containing a thick wad of papers. 'This is a copy of the entire collection of information we have on the Faroes – on unheaded paper, naturally. Please take from it what you need and then destroy everything. There are things written there we don't want left lying around.' He passed Bowman the envelope. 'I am trusting you to use any information in here with utmost discretion. There is no other way in which I can help you until you produce some evidence of your own from out there. Maybe you can take photographs or obtain some fresh information that we do not possess. Whatever: just get it to me.' As an afterthought he added: 'I hope you take heed of my warnings. The dangers are very real. If you were a member of my organisation I would not even consider allowing you to take on this little number. It isn't exactly insane, but it's damn close. I don't think it will work. Still, I have to admit, it's never been tried before, so we don't know.'

'Have you told anyone at *World-Watch* of this?' Bowman asked.

'No. I haven't even mentioned your name. In fact, when I leave here I will forget your name and just hope that we have not been seen together. One day, perhaps, when the time is right, I might get in touch with you. We might find a job for you.'

'When the time is right? When would that be?'

'People are already so much more aware of the fragility of our world. They care more, considerably more, than they did ten years ago. Just look at the impact the Greens have had in Germany. They are now where it counts; in their Parliament, in significant numbers. They are the voice of authority, respectable. We are moving in that direction, even though we have to crawl through mud to get there. The *right* time has not yet come to Britain; but it will you know, it really will.' He stood up and picked up his carry-all, just another fisherman off to his boat. The café was quiet now. 'Well, I must be away. I wish you good fishing.' He stooped down towards Bowman, briefly placing a hand on his shoulder, and said very quietly: 'It could be Man's last great cause you know, to rid the planet of those influences that seek to destroy it.'

Then he was gone, out into the rain that was now falling heavily. Bowman remained in the café for the next ten minutes, turning over in his mind everything Heath-Morton had said:

'one of the most dangerous activities in the western world.' After the gentleness and peace of the Lodge his thoughts were in turmoil. 'Dangerous', because they would call him a terrorist. But they, the people in power, were wrong. They were the ones who should be locked away, because they could not do their jobs properly, because they did not care enough for the future, because they lacked courage.

# 8

This would be his last run before taking *Hannah* down to Scotland. The weather was still a mess, squall after squall rushing from western quarters, increasing the time he had to spend at sea but, at least, hiding *Hannah* from those he wanted to avoid. The nights, also, were long enough for him to take the boat close in-shore and transfer the loads. It was April and the conditions were typical for the month. The wind gusted throughout the lengthening days only to fall for a few hours in the evening. This afforded Claus the chance of running in close to the caves on Esturoy or Streymoy, or the remoter fjords away from the Faroes' central region.

The worst of the weather was the mists. These hid *Hannah* visually, if not from radar, but Claus hated running close to rocks in the heaving seas. She had been a fine boat, serving him well through his smuggling years. She lived, all her curving wooden hull lived, and he had no desire to risk her on a Faroese reef. He had scraped her keel a few times as he had prowled the hazardous coastline; but he now knew the area as well as any man alive, though no one knew it well enough. On the Føroyar banks, in any boat, there was always risk.

Claus spat through the wheelhouse window. He could see only thirty or forty metres ahead. Glancing rapidly at the depth sounder, then the chart, he turned the helm slightly and *Hannah* nudged at dead slow against the tide. It was almost dark and yet the stark cliffs of Kunoy, a little off to the west, were barely visible, black against a deep grey sky.

'Jens,' he shouted, 'make sure everything is in the skip and stand by the anchor. It cannot be long now.' Jens waved and winched the skip's apparatus until the little boat was poised above the pitching seas on *Hannah*'s downwind flank.

Suddenly the depth reading moved from a steady eighty fathoms to less than forty. In that same moment the wind dropped as they moved under the lee of Kunoy, more clearly visible now that rain was not driving into their eyes. Claus watched the sounder's needle quiver. Thirty fathoms, and the wind was a pleasant breeze, the rain warm. *Hannah* thudded along, rolling in the groundswell.

There were no shore lights to guide them as the boat inched into Haraldssund, only Claus's knowledge, and the charts; but it was a good place to smuggle a load into the islands. Few people lived on Kunoy, and none at all anywhere near the landing place, four kilometres from the northern entrance to the sound. There was shelter from prevailing westerlies and no reefs in mid-channel, the steep sides of Kunoy, and Borðoy on the sound's east side, continuing deep down into the sea. But this was not a sailor's place, beneath the great lowering peak of Skarð, the waters like black, swirling ink. Claus knew that if he made a mistake in the wrong conditions *Hannah* would be sucked on to the hungry rocks.

He scoured the skyline for his trusted landmarks, boulders suspended on the mountainside. He found them and turned the boat so that she was running straight at Kunoy.

'Watch for surf, Jens. You should see it any moment.' His wiry, red-haired companion waved again, this time from up in the bows where he was already scanning the dark sea up ahead for the tell-tale sign of white water.

'Ja, it is there. I see it.' Jens loosed the anchor as Claus killed the engine. *Hannah* wallowed in the lumpy tide as the two men glanced anxiously along the shoreline. Now they ran their greatest risk, trapped in enclosed waters.

Together they winched down the heavily loaded skip.

'Mad bastards, us smugglers, eh Jens?' They laughed quietly, despite their nervousness. But this was the part they enjoyed most of all, even though there was always the terrible risk of being discovered while still at anchor. At any moment a fishery vessel could steam into the fjord, or a customs ship. Maybe the *Politi* were waiting on shore. Claus had his enemies, and there were those islanders who knew he was due for a run. Someone might have talked too loudly to the wrong person. That was always a chance.

They cast off and eased their oars into the water, pulling quietly and steadily. *Hannah* was anchored less than a hundred and fifty metres from the landing point, but they took several minutes to cross that distance. They listened as they pulled, straining to hear any unusual sound above the growling of the tide. Then the skip's keel grated on shingle and a wave rode them up on the beach.

'Now we work, Jens, and we must hurry,' whispered Claus. 'I do not like this place; it gives me a bad feeling.'

'It's land. Any land gives you bad feelings; you're like a fish.' Above them towered the mountains, just beyond the grassy slope which ran down to their little bay. The clouds were clearing and the moon silvered the wet rock. They were exposed to view to anyone who happened to be around, although that raw coastline appeared to be deserted.

'Come, we will take Bowman's materials first, and hide them in our own little cave.' They lifted the polythene-covered crate between them and hurried, so far as they were able with the weight of their burden, over the beach. Soon they were sweating as they struggled over half-seen rocks. They passed by the first two caves and climbed over some barnacle-encrusted boulders, resting occasionally only to adjust their load.

At last they reached the little cave that Claus had discovered on an earlier trip. It seemed perfect for their purpose, being quite apart from the caves they used for the islanders' cargo. Furthermore, it could only be seen from the sea and, even then, appeared insignificant compared with the big caves closer to the beach.

The cave's restricted size had its drawbacks. The two smugglers struggled with the crate as they man-handled it into the back of the rocky recess. Then they hid it, as best they could, with drift-wood, rocks and rotting weed. When they had finished they briefly flashed their red-lensed torches towards the back of the cave and it appeared to them as an innocent place, where seals might rest or give birth to their pups, but men would not venture.

Their muscles were trembling after their exertion, but they still had the islanders' goods to hide in one of the caves nearer the beach. Without hesitation they hurried back to the skip.

Often, they ran cargo with the help of their contacts on the islands. Off-loading, then, was accomplished in a matter of minutes, usually transferring while still at sea to fishing boats. The 'cave runs', however, they usually handled alone. They preferred them, even though they had to work harder and more slowly, and it meant leaving *Hannah* at anchor, because they disliked involving anyone else at that time, the most risky moment of their occupation. It was important, in particular, that this trip was unseen by any Faroese, so that they could hide the Englishman's materials.

It took them another twenty minutes to hide the islanders' load in the first of the big caves. They did not bother to cover up the goods. There was no need. Their contacts would arrive by boat from Esturoy before dawn. By daybreak the cave would be empty, the Esturoy boat apparently fishing away up the fjord and *Hannah* would be in Tórshavn, delivering her legal freight.

Their return trip to the anchored boat was fast, the skip being empty and the tide being with them. Back on board they half winched up the skip before starting the engine. Then they were away, turning out into the fjord. Soon they were like any other fishing boat that might have been sheltering from a squall. But Claus pushed *Hannah* on through the night, away from Kunoy Head and round into Kalsoyarfjörður and more open waters. He sent Jens below for some sleep and he sat alone at the helm.

This was a beautiful place, he thought, as the first light of dawn lit the seas off southern Esturoy; a sprawling coastline warmed by the Atlantic Drift, the snows on the mountains, and the grassy slopes bisected by rushing torrents. In a way he was looking forward to the summer, because the place was even more spectacular then and there was no darkness; but the risks then would be the greatest he had ever taken, especially in the continuous daylight. He hoped the Englishman was good. That would give them a chance.

# 9

George Albert Fitzgerald Junior, was like no other man Bowman had ever met, and neither had he known one he liked more.

The American pushed his heavy frame gingerly against the wall as he sat back on the cushioned box that served as a chair. 'Jees!' he announced. '*No one* lives like this in the States. What a dinky place you've found here, Son.' His big mouth grinned. 'Er, we are actually going to live here,Uh?'

'For the next few weeks, George, you're not going more than half a mile from this place.'

'Well, Son, just make sure there's plenty of Scotch.' He drained the glass which was enveloped in his thick grasp. Bowman threw him the bottle. 'I must be crazy. Why, oh why do I listen to you, leave my nice comfortable place in Oregon, where', he added with undisguised sarcasm, 'it is *dry* at this present time, and fly six thousand miles to Scotland, in winter? Damn,' he continued, 'did you know my father's grandparents were from this country?' Belligerently he glanced out of the window where the dusk and heavy rain cast a disquieting gloom over the wind-tossed loch.

'It's not winter, it's spring, and why is it that every American claims to have Scottish or Irish ancestry, never English or Welsh? Now shut up, you're jet-lagged and making even less sense than usual.'

Fitzgerald chuckled and shook his head. He appeared to be out of place in the Lodge, stooping his six feet three inches rather more than Bowman to avoid door lintels and the ceiling beams. Even sitting he seemed vast in the little rooms.

54

A savoury smell filled the room. Fitzgerald raised an eyebrow.

'It's haggis,' explained Bowman. 'Your Scottish ancestors would probably have lived on it.' The American groaned, and refilled his glass. The wind was picking up and the rain was now torrential, drops spattering in the fireplace. It was good to have company that night at Farewell, thought Bowman, particularly the huge, ponderous Fitzgerald. Despite his size he was somehow the antithesis of the all-American man; kind, jovial, lumbering; his thirty-five years carried with apparent care on his broad frame. He enjoyed, so he had told Bowman, playing 'football'. One wondered what sort of terrifying giant he would have appeared when padded out for a game. His great pride in life was his career which, as he described it, was 'doing anything that needed doing, so long as it was interesting'. He called himself an entrepreneur. He had made money, and lost most of it. When he lost he did not mind, provided he had learnt something.

Most of his money he had lost in the sea, for his passionate interest was in marine mammals. His friends had marvelled at the way he had backed his overwhelming enthusiasm with hard cash, some said millions of dollars, certainly hundreds of thousands. 'And I'd give the whole lot away to stop those bastards shooting-out the rest of the whales.' He had once shown Bowman a film he had taken while swimming with a blue whale, another giant, in the South Atlantic. 'Damn,' he had exclaimed as the huge animal stole across the screen. 'Two days after I shot this film, the Soviets harpooned her.' And you could see how much the memory hurt him, the way his massive frame tensed and his face lost its good-natured expression.

The way he was had also won and lost him two wives. They had been overpowered by his personality and his adventures; but they had gradually lost their admiration when he spent his fortunes on noble causes rather than on them. 'What the hell,' he would say; 'they were just Californian girls with more charms in their bodies than their brains.'

It had been more than a year since the two men had decided to pool their resources. Bowman's idea had seemed obvious to them in retrospect, although the details had taken so long to assemble.

It was a logical conclusion to have reached from the history of their interests and occupations, especially so when they considered their friendship with the Danish smugglers.

They were not going to involve themselves with conservation groups, or media exposure of a sensitive issue, or pour money into someone else's activities. They were not going to conform to anybody else's ideas or act by somebody else's will.

They were going to take a submarine into Faroese waters and use it to stop the whaling.

The storm raged outside the cottage as the two men ate. Bowman thought of the time when they had first met one another, on a lake called Leynarvatn, where the salmon were a legend, set among the rough mountains of Streymoy. He had seen the big American striding purposefully, his sandy hair in disarray, troll-like, along the shore towards where Bowman was sitting with a cup of coffee. 'Hi, I'm George Fitzgerald, mind if I join you for lunch?' It was hardly a question. He simply sat down in front of the Englishman and grinned. Fishing the high lakes of the Faroes, one did not expect to see another human being. While the country was engaging it was also lonely. Almost with relief one turned away and headed back to the villages, just for the sight of men and women. Thus their fascination with salmon and trout had brought the two men together in that wild and desolate place in the Faroes. Bowman did not consider himself a fatalist, but it was an extraordinary coincidence that the two of them should have met, especially there in the islands where both of them were to return, nine years after that first meeting.

The wind moaned through the heather on the hill above the Lodge. 'It reminds me of the storms we get in British Columbia during the Fall,' said Fitzgerald. 'Hell, the wind screams through those islands, straight off the Pacific. Come to think of it, maybe there are a few guys who live in places like this up there; but most folk head on down to Washington or Oregon in winter. Columbia's a wilderness.' Abruptly he changed the subject: 'Son, do you reckon we got a chance?'

'A good chance; especially with Claus and Jens, and *Hannah*.' Not that it was an important consideration, a condition, any more. They were committed, so long as there was a fragment of a chance. Bowman knew that the American had been committed a year ago, even as they were developing the plan, even when it had appeared to be impulsive and far-fetched, too adventurous to have a hope of success. But there was a good chance. There were, as Vicky had insisted, so many things that could go wrong, over which they had little or no control. The sea itself, in that northern latitude, would give problems enough, even for a boat on the surface. But, yes, Bowman knew that even had there been almost no chance at all of success, Fitzgerald was committed; because of his acute sense of right and wrong, and most of all because of his love for those great sea mammals of Føroyar. Furthermore, while it had been Bowman's idea to use a submarine, it had been Fitzgerald's to try tapes of whale sonar to guide the pilot whales offshore, away from the hunters. They had to test their system.

Both men recognised the magnitude of their commitment. Their future was now irrevocably entwined with the venture. The past was gone, important only in what influence it had had on their beliefs, and they strove through the present towards their chosen goals, even to find a meaning for being alive, a value. And the future was the terrifying unknown that repelled and yet drew them, a battle with their fears, their nightmares and weaknesses, so that they each might earn no more than the right to live with a clear conscience.

'Crazy,' said Fitzgerald suddenly, 'utterly crazy.' He looked at the Englishman. 'How long we got, before Claus gets here?'

'A month at the most, if he hasn't been caught smuggling.' Fitzgerald laughed as he thought of the Danes running their illegal freight around the North Atlantic.

'Hell of a life!' He shook his head in wonderment. Then he asked: 'What do they run nowadays?'

'I'm not sure, they keep quiet about that. I only know they never run alcohol or dope. Neither', Bowman added, 'have they ever had a submarine in *Hannah*'s hold.'

On the mention of the boat's name the two men again fell silent and remembered the times they had spent with the Danes, fishing and whale-watching in waters from North Norway to Iceland to the Faroes banks. It was, as Fitzgerald said, a hell of a way to spend a life; smuggling in winter, during the long, dark nights, then running legal cargo and fishing during summer, while exposed by the perpetual daylight of those high northern latitudes. But it was a grand life and both Fitzgerald and Bowman knew that neither Dane would swap it for any other.

Bowman thought of that other strange coincidence that had resulted in their meeting the Danes. He and Fitzgerald had wanted to take a break from salmon fishing on the island lakes and had made inquiries in Vestmanna harbour as to whether there was a boat and crew which might take them out to where they could fish for cod, or maybe porbeagle shark. *Hannah* was in harbour and they had been directed towards her. They never saw a porbeagle, Bowman mused, but Claus Hansen had shown them a lot of whales.

Fitzgerald was remembering those whales, the dense schools of pilots, hundreds of dark shapes curling on the surface; the immense finback whales, almost as big as blues, with their roaring blows that shot higher than *Hannah*'s main-mast; and the orcas, the killers, most spectacular of all, overtaking the boat in a flash, turning back as if to ram, cracking their black tails on the waves and reaching their heads out of the sea to gain a better view.

And both men remembered the whalers: the way the Faroese boats herded all those animals into shallow waters, and the long spears smashed down into the black backs; the terrible screams echoing around the bays, and the long blood signature seeping three miles out to sea. Bowman remembered seeing the big American with tears in his eyes when they had witnessed that, heard those agonising cries of frightened and dying whales . . .

Worst of all was the way the hunters left the babies until last, until the mother whales had bled to death and all you could hear were little cries; but they filled your ears and you never forgot them.

'This just *has* to work, Son,' said Fitzgerald. 'We got to get the submarine among those whales and direct them away from the whaling bays. It's some heavy order, but we've got to do it.'

'It's not getting the submarine in close enough that is worrying me,' replied Bowman; 'I only hope that the sonar will make the whales do what we want them to.'

'You let me worry about that.'

'And there's something else we ought to worry about.' Bowman told the American of the meeting with Heath-Morton in Inverness. Fitzgerald frowned. They were convinced that so far as the submarine was concerned the main problem was in building and testing it within a few weeks; but they agreed that provided they had not overlooked anything in the materials direction it was possible to assemble a working submersible craft. They were confident the Danes would not let them down. It was the unknown human factors which preyed on their minds. Who followed Bowman in Inverness? What organisation or government departments sought to destroy the Green Movement throughout Europe, and groups like *World-Watch*? Who was it that really frightened men like Heath-Morton? It was more than secret services or ordinary right-wingers. Heath-Morton had been emphatic with his warning. They had far more than the Faroese to fear.

Beneath the pilot whales the squid were so tightly packed as to form a sonar screen from the sea bed. North-west of the little island of Koltur, in Vágafjörður, the whales fed, and the sea tingled with the crackle of their echo-location. But the school was more than feeding, it was splitting. The older animals were drifting southward on the tide, together with some of the younger whales which would form a new school when the old ones died. During the day the leader of the main school ceased

59

to call out his unifying sonar. There was disorder. The whales spread, until by dusk there appeared to be no single school, just hundreds of animals over a large area of sea.

Then, in the twilight, the leader called.

His song was different, it had evolved; fewer of the listening whales were attracted to it. Another big male was calling, and his voice competed with the old leader. The callers were four kilometres apart. In darkness order returned; two schools had formed, farther and farther apart until one could not hear the other and they were distinct, isolated groups.

One, the main part of the original school, was awash off Stakkarnir Head, close inshore, drifting. The other was swimming fast, even the old whales driving hard at the currents spilling through Hest Fjörður. This school turned west, away from Streymoy and headed towards open sea beyond Sandoy.

This was just one of the many social functions which the pilot whales performed each year on the Faroes banks. The archipelago was where the schools met, merged or split, where new orders came from the old; quietly, calmly, and with the wisdom of many past generations.

# 10

In the good weather that followed the storms of March and early April, the two men at Farewell Lodge worked to the limit of their physical ability. From the barn adjacent to the cottage exuded a near-permanent smell of catalyst-set reinforced plastic. Bowman hoped that no one would be walking near by and notice the smell. If someone did happen to pass then he and Fitzgerald were going to excuse the smell by claiming that they were building a new boat for the loch. This was plausible, he thought; for the old wooden boat leaked dangerously, her timber being too rotten to be worth repair. Difficulties would develop only if an inquisitive visitor asked to see the work in progress, for the boat being built in the barn's shelter bore little resemblance to a traditional loch boat. In the days that passed, however, even the shepherd was not seen. Fitzgerald noticed a fishing boat one morning, away down the loch, and this was apparently the closest anyone came to seeing the peculiar construction at Farewell Lodge.

She was five metres in length and nearly three in width; her raw, white and grey sections loosely assembled after their recent removal from the wood and plaster moulds. The grey in the sections appeared like a net meshwork against the white. This was a wrap of carbon fibre which would enable the boat to dive more than twice as deep, and absorb greater shocks, than if she had been built in glass-fibre alone.

'She looks the part,' said Fitzgerald as they admired this stage of their creation: the wedge nose and the bulbous body tapered to a flattish curve at the stern; the short extensions, which would house enclosed propellers, like turbines, on each

61

side. There were also arms extending behind the boat which would hold her elevation and steerage rudders.

'That was the easy part,' replied Bowman. They had been working on the boat for a little over a week and they both knew that though they had prepared the bulkiest components for the submarine's shell, the electrical work and finishing processes would take longer and be more difficult. Bowman was anxious. He had assembled and tested small submersibles for too many years to deceive himself now as to the complexity of their task. A boat that would lie and manoeuvre even at ten fathoms required precise attention to the strength of its hull. It demanded absolute confidence in every part of its structure and design. Working in powerful currents, like those in the North Sea, or in island and channel waters, necessitated powerful, efficient, electric motors and a hydrodynamic hull. All these, thought Bowman, were going to take time and extreme care to accomplish to the necessary standard. A mistake was too terrifying to contemplate. A submariner never thinks of a ruptured hull, or exhausted engines, or air leaks; not, anyway, while diving. It was before submerging that you worried about such things. So you tested every centimetre of the hull with pressure-drivers and water jets. You built in extra wiring and, most of all, you over-designed the positive-ballast system, doubling up the air lines, both to the flotation tanks and the cabin. More than anything, a submarine had to be a water-tight chamber, built, in the first instance, to float. This was the overriding rule. If it lost its ability to surface, it was a coffin.

Despite his racing thoughts, Bowman was impressed by the boat's lovely curves. She did indeed look as if currents would spill over her, like a dolphin's body, rather than hit her at full force, halting her progress. Even the outer buoyancy tanks were no more than ridges along the hull's flanks. He loved beautifully designed machines, especially boats. This, he ruminated, was why he had worked so long for the oil company. He had had virtually unlimited access to new materials and designs, and the ability to test his creations, first in the shallow research pools; then off the rigs, in the black depths of the

North Sea. This time there would be no pools, just the cold waters of Loch Farewell, and then the Faroes banks.

Bowman watched as Fitzgerald set to work on sanding each section as smooth as possible before the final glass-fibre skin could be applied. The American worked with extreme care, for Bowman had impressed on him the value of the carbon net that was woven hard into the glass. Over-sanding would spoil the integrity of this reinforcement and would build a weakness into the hull. Too little sanding would result in ridges that would substantially reduce the craft's hydrodynamics, spoiling her efficiency and making her noisy. Fitzgerald's gloved hands rubbed away at the reinforced plastic and Bowman admired the way the big man took such dextrous care. To do an important job, something that was difficult and required so much care, you had to have the best people, those who believed absolutely in the value of what they were trying to pull off. Bowman had the Danes and the American, and the Professor back in London. He could not imagine having four better people.


Gradually the boat's shape took on a greater solidity. The seals between each joint were designed for rapid assembly and disassembly. There was a silicon-greased strip of soft polymer between each section, compressed between flattened aluminium strips, clip-bolted every six inches. The sections were as large as was practically possible, to keep the number of seals to a minimum. Seals and joints were always the weakest points of any boat.

'What'll we call her?' inquired Bowman one evening.

'I've been wondering about that,' replied Fitzgerald. 'What was it that Cervantes called Don Quixote's old pack horse?'

'Trusted steed, you mean. *Rozinante*. Yes, that would be appropriate. We are, after all, about as crazy as the old knight. It fits somehow, doesn't it?'

'It fits.'

And so the boat, given her name, took on a personality.

Every other day Bowman travelled across the loch and then, by the Land Rover, into the nearest village, which was fourteen miles away, for stores and to collect any letters. The old lady in the Post Office, which doubled as a general stores, always eyed him with suspicion.

'Ye seem a wee bit airly for the troot,' she would say, by way of inquiring as to how he was spending his time at the Lodge.

'Well, I'm not doing very much fishing. There's plenty of work to do on the cottage.' Then he would talk about the weather, a subject which was very dear to her heart, or describe how he was renovating the old beams and mortar work. He also let it casually slip that he was repairing an old glass-fibre boat for when the wooden one became too unsound for use on the loch.

Towards the end of April the parcel he had been expecting from London arrived.

'I'll no be lifting that above the counter. Ye'll have tae come aroond here and pick it up yerself.' It was, indeed, heavy, though not more so than he had expected. He rushed the package back to the Lodge, anxious to see how the Professor had tackled the complicated problem of the sonar equipment. He found Partridge's scrawled letter among the polystyrene granules with which the apparatus was protected.

Dear Richard,

        I have done what you asked, you scoundrel, and when they know it was I who built it I expect they will put me in the same prison cell as you.

The transmitter/receiver *must* be placed as far away as possible from any source of noise or vibration. With the syntax you gave me you will see a circle on your monitor representing the sweep area around the device. You can vary the range, although accuracy will rapidly fall off for most objects at distances greater than a mile. The only differentiation between objects that I can build in is between hard and soft objects. The size of the object is represented by the size of its signal. You will get used to it and you can adjust the calibration yourself, provided you remember anything of what I taught you. This will give you an intuitive understanding of the machine.

Depth of the object is shown alongside the illuminated pixels by a +, − or 0. + tells you that the object is above the receiver, 0 implies same depth, while − suggests a deeper echo. Obviously, I have screened out the background of the sea-bed. The depth of water directly beneath the machine will be shown, in feet, at the bottom right of the screen. At the top right will be shown the depth of water above the machine, i.e. the depth at which it is operating.

If you gave me longer I could build in certain other brilliant niceties; but, no, you are in a hurry as usual! One thing you must remember is that while the device is on 'passive', i.e. just receiving, you will only see on the screen circle a significant noise source such as another sonar device. This will be the most unreliable of the machine's modes as it is so difficult in shallow water, as you know, to interpret directional signals. Sounds appear to come from all directions. The signals might jump around the screen until you switch to short range: a hundred metres.

Good luck, scallywag, whatever it is you are up to. Come and see me when it is all over. Vicky is coming to stay with me while you are away, so you have no need to worry. This adventure of yours had better be worth the unhappiness you are causing that fine girl.

Yours ever,

Prof.


As Bowman knew it would be, the device was beautifully simple and robustly constructed. He had no doubts, however, about how complex the program was that Partridge had loaded on the two compact floppy discs which had been packed with the hardware. Furthermore, the Professor had made the device in sections that could be connected rapidly by watertight plugs. The transmitter/receiver was sealed in a curve-faced box. This would be fitted in the nose of *Rozinante*. Two wires led from there to the signal amplification and analysis unit which was connected in turn to the power source and to the computer and monitor.

The job of fitting the device into the boat, which Bowman had imagined would have needed several days, had in fact been completed by six in the evening of that same day.

'George, I feel better about this business than at any time since we dreamt it up.'

'You just enjoy playing around with machines. Now that your little creation here has her "nervous system", you're a happier man. I'll be a lot better disposed to it when I see it working.'

'It'll work. You don't know the Professor.'


Then they worked for almost eighteen hours a day. There were few hours when one or other of them was not in the barn. While the sonar device had been easily fitted, there were problems with the motors and transmission. Bowman wanted the motors to be outboard, with a nylon gearing system direct to the propellers. Cooling the motors was the problem. He and Fitzgerald eventually resolved the difficulty by taking an air line from the cabin to the motors on each of the arms and then ducting the air, under sufficient pressure to keep the wiring cool, back into the cabin.

'At least it will keep us warm,' suggested Bowman.

'Yeah, and if the motors' wiring burns out we'll be poisoned by the fumes.'

'You're a pessimist, George.'

'A realist, Son, just a crazy realist.'


On the sixth of May the *Rozinante* had reached the stage when she could be taken out on the loch for her first tests. As the last of the light dwindled in the western sky the two men began transferring the sections to the ramp by the shore. It took less than an hour to assemble the boat, make fast and double-check all the seal-clips, and load and connect all the equipment. The boat was powered by only three of her full complement of twelve heavy-duty, lead-acid batteries. As the batteries were also part of the submarine's ballasting, Bowman and Fitzgerald compensated the lack of battery weight with the equivalent in bags of gravel.

In the near darkness on the western shore of Loch Farewell there were no outsiders to see the launch of the strange vessel. Fitzgerald pushed her clear of the bank while Bowman, alone on board, allowed the motors to run at slow reverse. He was peculiarly detached as he watched the shore recede and felt the loch's gentle swell rock the *Rozinante*. The motors hummed quietly as he turned the boat out into the darkness. He looked at the monitor's red glow. Everything appeared to be working. The depth below registered as eighty feet. He stopped the motors, pulled the hatch down and fastened the eight clip-bolts. Opening the air valve he heard the reassuring hiss in the sealed cabin. He was nervous then, as before any dive he had ever made. This time it was worse; because of the dark and because there had not been the independent string of rigorous safety checks. His thoughts raced over the submarine's design, the seals, the glass-fibre, the motors, the air supply and its back-up.

He switched the sonar on to a hundred metres. There was a fuzz on the western side of the monitor's circle. That was the shore, as it should have been. The rest of the circle was empty until, soon, a speck appeared, also from the west. This was Fitzgerald in the ferry boat. Partridge's sonar was working. He checked the air pressure, the seals again and the condition of the batteries. The depth below him was now ninety feet. With the motors off he opened the positive ballast valve and the tanks began to flood.

Fitzgerald, just a few metres away as the valves opened, watched the *Rozinante* fall. In a moment she was gone, leaving a swirling bulge of water at the surface. She was like a whale, he thought; elusive, seeking sanctuary and peace in the deep. Then there was nothing, only the gently rolling waves.

Bowman's heart was racing as he closed the valves and immediately pumped air back into the tanks to halt the boat's descent. The hull sections creaked as the pressure built up, then there was only the hiss of air again. The screen told him that he was twenty feet below the surface. A mere twenty feet, that was nothing, he told himself. He could still throw off the hatch and would survive the blast of cold water. The sudden pressure would not kill him at that depth. He was hypnotised by the screen in front of him. The boat steadied at twenty-five feet.

He was near panic. This was worse even than his very first dive off the rigs. There had been others with him then, and a tried and tested submarine. Here he was surrounded by black water in which, through the narrow strips of Perspex windows, he could see nothing. He was poised above nearly seventy feet of water and everything was so still. He breathed deeply, but he could feel the thump of his heart even as he listened to the hiss of air in the cabin, and the occasional burst of bubbles leaving the escape valve. Quickly he looked around his cocoon and inspected the seals. They were dry. It was all right, he kept telling himself; everything was holding together. There was plenty of air, the *Rozinante* was stable.

For five minutes he did no more than pump and release air from the ballast tanks, maintaining the boat's trim at about twenty-five feet. Gradually he relaxed. The central part of the screen circle was clear except for the single speck and a plus sign: Fitzgerald. The rest was a fuzz, emptiness; there was nothing else within a hundred metres. The three batteries were almost completely charged. The boat's nose was pointing north, the direction in which, he knew, there were two miles of open water. He suddenly remembered to switch on the forward flood-lamp so that Fitzgerald would know where he was. Then he started the motors at dead slow.

The *Rozinante* eased ahead and Bowman felt nothing. The depth began to increase until he levelled the elevation rudder. His course remained north at a mere half a knot. He noticed that the speck, now in the bottom half of the screen, was stationary, showing that Fitzgerald could see the flood-light and was following. Now he was relaxed and felt in control. He opened the motors to half speed.

Then he could feel the foam rubber of the seat push at his back. He steered the boat a few points to the east and then back to the west. The compass needle wavered and the boat rocked slightly, creaked and settled to her course. Bowman shut down the port motor and the *Rozinante* turned. The needle eased through nearly 180 degrees until he shut down the starboard engine. All the instruments were steady; he was stationary at twenty-six feet. Again he opened the ballast valve and the boat dropped deeper, very slowly, creaking as the pressure built-up. Bowman felt sweat dripping from his eyebrows.

And then there was a bang.

Instinctively, even as he waited for the terrible smash of cold water and the crushing blow of high pressure, Bowman closed the ballast valve and opened the air line into the tanks to maximum. But the cabin was dry. The boat lay at forty-five feet. One of the panels had distorted, not cracked. Bowman rubbed his hands over his face. It happened all the time in glass-fibre boats; panels buckling slightly under the pressure. You got used to it; you had to if you dived to any depth.

Fitzgerald's boat appeared on the screen to be virtually dead ahead. Bowman opened the motors, slowly building up the speed towards three-quarters. *Rozinante* began to vibrate and the motors hummed. He could hear them quite distinctly. There was another thud and he tensed, but soon relaxed; another panel 'going concave' as submariners referred to it. Then the vibration was quite intense and Bowman dared not open the motors any further.

He was using a lot of the meagre battery power now, surging through the water at a depth of forty feet. He was bringing her up with the elevation rudder, without airing the ballast tanks. He watched Fitzgerald's speck become almost coincident with the screen's centre, but the plus sign, and his own depth, showed that the wooden boat was a comfortable distance above him.

When the speck drifted below the screen's centre, Bowman shut the motors down, aired the tanks and surfaced. He was shaking as the vague light of the surface showed through the viewing windows, and he could hear the waves again. He threw open the hatch and gulped in the cool air.

Later, back in the Lodge, the *Rozinante* disassembled and stored in the barn, Bowman still shook as Fitzgerald poured him another Scotch.

'She works, George,' he said excitedly; 'she works so well.'

'Yeah, she worked this time; but we still got to see how she operates in the salt, in powerful tides.'

'She'll be fine. We'll have to put extra supports on those motor arms though; she vibrates like hell at three-quarters speed. In powerful currents we might have to run her at full power. At the moment that would tear off the motors.' He slapped Fitzgerald on the back and laughed loudly. 'But she *works*, George.'

The next morning, as he walked between the cottage and the barn, Bowman happened to look across the loch towards where the Land Rover was parked. He stopped and stared, wondering what he had seen. It came again, a flash of glass in the sunlight. He hurried back into the cottage.

'There's someone watching us from across the loch,' he told Fitzgerald. 'I saw the flash of binoculars.' Both men looked out of the window. 'It was near the Land Rover, on the hill just above.' There was nothing to be seen.

'Locals, maybe, inquisitive as to what we're about.'

'It's seven-thirty; a bit early for interested villagers to take a peep at us.'

'Well, let's go take a look at them,' suggested Fitzgerald.

They were across the loch in five minutes. During the crossing they watched the approaching shore, but saw nothing. They walked up the hill above their vehicle.

'It must have been a bird or something, George. There's no one here.'

Then Fitzgerald pointed out the butt of a cigarette on the ground. He looked around them at the sprawl of heather, rocks and stunted birch. 'And I got the strangest feeling just now, Son, that we're being watched. I tell you there's someone up there right now.' He nodded in the direction of the hills which reached away above them, rolling towards the mountain at the head of the loch.

'I got no explanations,' said the American, 'but who the hell is it out there?'

# 11

'They've been here,' said Fitzgerald as he hurried into the cottage. 'Some bastard's been in the barn and had a snoop around.'

Bowman rushed out, following the American. 'Is anything gone?'

'Just disturbed. Whoever it was has had a good look over the boat. I can't see any damage.'

The two men inspected the barn and submarine. Tools had been moved, boxes pushed over and *Rozinante*'s hatch opened. Doubtless the intruders had been inside the boat.

'There was more than one man here,' suggested Bowman. 'It would have taken at least two to move those boxes quietly, without disturbing us.'

'How the hell did they get here? We would have heard a boat coming across.'

'They probably came over the hill, from the track at the top of the loch.' He rubbed the stubble on his face. 'There's no more time, George; we'll have to finish up here immediately and get the boat to Claus.'

*Home Office MI5 –Section C*

Ref. SW Conservation/Terrorist 3324

Running investigation: Bowman, Richard; Fitzgerald, George.

Together in Bowman's cottage in Scotland. The men have nearly completed the building of a miniature submarine. Prospective use unknown. Under 24 hour surveillance by Burrows and Hamilton, Section E. No contact with outside world except via outgoing letters and incoming letters and parcels collected from PO at village; Brocness. No visitors. No phone connected.

Bowman and Fitzgerald are alerted to the presence of our watchers.

*File Running.*

Willoughby slammed his fist on the table as he finished reading the report. He had stamped *High Priority* on the directive, and they had continued the investigation at middle level. They should have bugged the cottage and examined the letters. Then they would know by now exactly what Bowman and Fitzgerald were preparing to do. As it was, C Section was in the dark. The operatives had the excuse, of course, that they were working in the difficult countryside of Northern Scotland; but there were always excuses.

So for what purpose were the men building a submarine? Reactor outflows? Greenpeace had done that; monitored the radiation from underwater exhaust pipes from Sellafield. And that had resulted in more than an embarrassment for the government and the CEGB. Bowman and Fitzgerald might be targeting another reactor; Dungeness, maybe, or the fast breeder at Dounray. Why else would conservationists need a submersible boat? Obviously they wanted to work unobserved. Perhaps a terrorist attack on shipping?

He wondered about informing Head of Section. There was no need. He would read the file in any case. Why draw it to his attention. This was Willoughby's operation. What to do next? The submarine was nearly completed. It could be assumed, therefore, that the subjects would begin their activities in the near future. He could let them begin and then drop on them

73

while in the act . . . But what if their operation were abroad? He would then have to pass the file over to Foreign Office and would lose it. He would never even learn the outcome. Of course, it was *just* possible that the subjects were not building their machine for any illegal purpose. Perhaps they were going to film underwater.

He opened a new *High Priority* directive. 'Sabotage the submarine. Monitor conversations. Report every 24 hours.'


But Willoughby was too late.


The tiny natural harbour, sheltered in a steep-sided gorge cutting in from the open sea, was empty. The rough track that had led away from the road three miles away faded out on the shingle of the beach, where the Land Rover, with its trailer in tow, came to a halt. It was mid-May and even at one in the morning there was still light in the sky. Bowman and Fitzgerald did not hesitate in their clandestine activities. They had reduced the time for assembly of the submarine to less than twenty anxious minutes. They would have taken their watchers by surprise, moving late in the evening; but now, on the beach, they were completely exposed. They were sure, however, that no vehicle had followed them away from the road.

Fitzgerald, sweating, heaved the *Rozinante* off the gravel until she was floating. Bowman, dressed in a wet suit, climbed into the cabin.

'Well, this is it, Son, our boat begins her journey,' said Fitzgerald. 'Take care and I'll see you in a couple of hours. Signal me if you're in trouble; I'll be watching from the cliffs.' He clapped Bowman on the shoulder.

The Englishman smiled, a little nervously Fitzgerald thought.

'Shove me off George, let's get this boat away before our friends find where we are.'

Within a few minutes the *Rozinante* was at the entrance to the harbour, still on the surface, and pushing quietly out to sea. Bowman sealed down the hatch and examined the instruments. He was nervous, but much more confident with the boat now, even though they had not had adequate time to test her in powerful tides. No lights showed out to sea. The depth fell to forty feet. He would run on the surface for as long as it was safe, he decided. The boat could travel much faster on top of a smooth sea. Away from the cover of the cliffs he would be too visible on the surface and would need to dive. He held her on a course due north, out into the Atlantic. A hundred feet now lay below the boat and the swell rolled her. The motors turned at a third of their power, at which they were most efficient, conserving the batteries, running the boat at nearly three knots.

Bowman had the sonar switched to a mile range. The coast appeared as a hard line towards the bottom of the screen. Nothing showed up ahead, the ocean appeared to be empty. Slowing the motors, he flooded the ballast tanks and dived. Soon the sea's surface was unmarked.

Fitzgerald, high on the cliffs, had watched as the half-seen, half-imagined shape dwindled. If anyone happened to be near by and looking out to sea, the mysterious, figment shape that had been cruising on the surface was a shoal of fish or flock of birds, or perhaps a family of seals; unless, of course, the watchers knew of the existence of the submarine. Now, anyway, it was gone.

Two miles off-shore the *Hannah* stole through the night, heading west along the coast of Scotland, as she had done for the previous two nights, and would do at least until Bowman made his move. Claus was tired. The previous day Customs officers in Scrabster harbour had thoroughly searched the boat and questioned him for hours as to why he was requesting to stay in British waters. He had made the excuse that he and Jens needed to do some work and tests on their engine before resuming fishing in the Norwegian Sea. The Customs officers had even turned over the frozen fish in the hold, taking a few away with them to examine. Maybe they suspected he was a smuggler. If they thought that, then naturally they would be looking for drugs. They did not really care about anything else, especially in Britain. You could smuggle in a car, and they would not notice; but they would sniff out a few pounds of cannabis. That was good, thought Claus. A car did not matter; it was a bit of fun and not very much money. But running drugs made ruthless men rich, while they ruined people – in the way that alcohol was killing the Faroese cargo workers and fishermen.

It was a cloudy night and warm, a gentle southerly blowing off the mainland. Claus continually glanced towards the open sea to the north and checked the radar for any shipping. They had seen some fishing boats earlier, and a big freighter, but no fishery protection vessels or Customs launches. He was not over-worried that *Hannah* was being shadowed. She had been too well searched in Scrabster. Customs would not be particularly concerned with the trawler any more. Dope-runners did not smuggle the stuff out of Britain; it was a one-way market. Besides, the coast of Scotland was a massive area to police.

'There,' called Jens, urgently, from the bows. 'The signal, it is there.'

Claus had seen the flashing light in the water and was already turning *Hannah* in towards shore. He cut the engine when the boat was within two hundred metres of the light. *Hannah* was adrift. He and Jens watched the distant hills for any unusual sign. They both knew this was pointless, that if Customs were on to them it was already too late. But he trusted Bowman to have chosen the area with extreme care.

Still nothing showed on the radar. They saw the vague shape of a distant tanker on the horizon, but there was nothing close by on the surface. Again the light flashed in the water, now only thirty yards off.

'They have done it, Jens; they have built a submarine.' Suddenly the *Rozinante* surfaced among a surge and billow of bubbles, the hatch opened and the Danes were staring into Bowman's grinning face. Claus spoke, just loudly enough for

76

the Englishman to hear. 'Ja, clever bastard. Now we stow that boat, eh, and get away from here.'

The three men worked quickly, after the briefest of greetings. Soon they had straps around the submarine and were winching her on board, even as Bowman was unclipping the sections. In ten minutes Claus and Jens had stowed the machinery below, beneath the fish-hold.

As the Danes clamped down the hatch, Bowman was pulling on flippers and an air tank, and routinely spitting into his face mask. He felt peculiarly light-headed.

'Someone knows about the submarine. We don't know who it is, but it's probably some Home Office department. Get her away quickly. We'll see you in Vikarfjord on Wednesday,' he called as *Hannah*'s engine restarted. Claus and Jens waved as Bowman dropped overboard into the dark sea. Then the trawler was making full speed away from the coast, out towards international waters; and the Englishman was alone, shutting from his mind the horrors of the depths below him, thinking only of the luminous compass needle on his wrist, and kicking steadily towards the south.

**12** Heading north-west, *Hannah* rode the easy swell. Away to the west the little island of North Rona crouched against the sea. The Danes stood together in the wheelhouse, watching the fugitive beauty of the early morning sky.

But Claus Hansen was not really thinking of the fine weather. The weeks ahead were going to be dangerous, because of the problems they were bound to encounter. Firstly in smuggling the submarine into its hiding place and then in moving it, and Bowman and Fitzgerald, quickly around the scattered Faroese coastline avoiding undue attention, and dropping the boat wherever they found whales. There would be no darkness now, in Faroes, until the end of August. They would have to hope for mists and poor weather.

Jákup Poulsen would be the greatest danger of them all, because of the hatred that was so intense between him and Hansen, because of Eidi, and because of the whaling. Poulsen would do anything, Claus knew, to destroy him. The *Stormur*, Poulsen's boat, was fast, and the only Faroese whaler armed with a harpoon cannon.

'You are thinking of Jákup?' asked Jens who had noticed the strange look on his friend's face.

'Always, when we are bound for Føroyar I think of Jákup, and my Eidi. He's a bad bastard, Jens; meanest man I ever met.'

'He frightens you.'

'His cruelty, his ignorance frighten me. He has not the mind of an ordinary man, there is no reason in him, and yet he is a hero among his people. To him the killing is everything. But really I am frightened for his sister, my Eidi. He has too strong a hold over her. While he lives she will never leave the islands. She thinks she can control his evil, and that no one else can.'

'It is true perhaps; that no one else can control him.'

'Ja, but neither can she.'

For a few minutes they were quiet, then Jens said, 'Now a new whaling season has begun. Jákup will be happy.' Claus spat out of the wheelhouse window.

'We are going to meet this summer. We will end it, one way or another.'


Jákup Poulsen was deliriously happy. He was sobbing with joy as he stood on the *Stormur*'s harpoon platform. A kilometre off-shore, in Vágafjörður, the whaler had turned around a school of pilot whales and was heading them back towards the whaling beach at Miðvágur. A line of boats showed up ahead against the sunrise as the islanders formed a barrier to the whales, guiding them in-shore as the *Stormur* gave chase. Poulsen shouted towards the wheelhouse, frantically signalling the helmsman to steer to starboard, so that the whales would be hemmed in against the wall of fishing boats. None must escape; he hated losing whales.

The great beasts surged at the surface, confused by the sudden noises, of propellers and of oars beating on the sea, of strange sonar that was obscuring their own, making it difficult to differentiate the leader's voice among the chaos of sound. They were frightened, travelling as one unit in the direction where there was least noise. In their school there were more than three hundred individuals.

The whales rounded Presttangi, the Priest's Point, and were directed into the confines of the little fjord by the beating oars and shouting men and boys in the string of boats. They began to panic and turn back towards the noises that frightened them, but Poulsen had timed his moment well. He signalled dead-ahead and the *Stormur* ran in among the whales. He was laughing, his eyes and mouth wide open; and he could see the whale backs clearly over the sights of the cannon. This was *his* moment; the shot which would be the first kill of the year. He drew it out, allowing the backs to slide out of view into the blue depths; one, then another, and another. He watched the whales' great, bulbous heads just beneath the surface, their long pectoral fins, and their tails driving them along. He could see that they were already tired; the big, old males, and the females with calves close in to their flanks.

Beneath the gun a mother and calf surfaced, almost in the centre of the school. From Poulsen's throat came a half-choked groan of pleasure, while the muscles in his face were taut as an almost sexual joy enveloped him. He eased the line of sight from the female's back to her head, and he squeezed the trigger.

The untethered harpoon flew and struck in the whale's neck, just missing the spine and embedding itself eighteen inches deep in her flesh. She half-lunged at the surface, the tearing pain scorching down her back. Her tail smashed against her little calf. Suddenly, for a long moment, there was no other sound but a single, drawn-out scream. Then a dreadful second of shock and silence as a swell broke red against the *Stormur*'s bows and the great beast spun in the sea. Poulsen was on his knees as, gradually, a bellowing laugh escaped from his stretched mouth, and the islanders in the boats cheered. The *grind* had begun.

Once the first whale had been injured, there was no hope for a single member of the school, for it was quite impossible for them to leave one of their number in distress. She screamed and they milled around her, terrified yet unable to abandon her. The calf was on the surface, blinded by her mother's blood. Again there was noise, all around them as the boats closed in and darkened the skyline.

One boat, powered by rowing men, steered in among them. In the bows stood a man waving a whale hook, a barbed curve of iron attached to a rope. As the boat rammed the injured female, the hunter drove the hook into her head, and he too, like Poulsen, experienced the tingling surge of utter joy as the whale's muscles convulsed and she broached the sea; and she screamed again.

Under tow from the rowing boat, the bleeding whale had ceased to struggle, though she was not yet dead. Her calf followed immediately behind, and then the rest of the school, blindly following the new, macabre pilot. Behind the whales were the rest of the boats, forty in number, and finally, standing off to sea, the *Stormur*. The beasts all cried their fear, but it was nothing as yet.

In the shallows off Miðvágur village the whales threshed the sea, and the boats were among them, men poised with harpoons and spears, blades nearly two feet long, and big hooks. Almost in unison the men lunged, throwing all their weight on to the spear shafts, into the backs and heads of the *grindvhal*. The screams now filled the air and sea, and the foaming water was scarlet. All the baby whales cried, but their voices were too weak to be heard among the greater sounds of terror and agony, the thud and tearing of blades and *grind* hooks, and the frenzied shouts of men. The spears struck again and again, deep into flesh, sometimes into spines; now gashing across a flank, laying bare crimson flesh; then into a whale's eye.

Jákup Poulsen had transferred from the *Stormur* on to one of the small boats. He was in among the whales, driving his notched spear hard at his targets. Whale blood gushed across his chest and face and he laughed in delight. The sickly smell of hot blubber filled the air, but it was the sweetest smell of all to Jákup, and those screams were more beautiful than any other sound to him.

The word was out among the islands: there was a *grind* at Miðvágur. The Vágar islanders drove by car to the little harbour to see and help in the kill. Soon there were a thousand people watching the whaling bay. More boats arrived, and still more cars, and a ferry boat stood out at the entrance to the bay. Then visitors arrived from the other islands. Three hours after Poulsen had shot the first whale the cries were still being heard. Men were still driving in the spears.

Whales were being dragged up the beach as teams of men pulled on the *grind*-hook ropes. Some of the creatures were dead, others flopped weakly as the hooks bit deeply into their flesh. One by one all but the heaviest were hauled from the water. The foremen of the *grind*, bearing their long, decorative knives, walked among the carcasses and crying beasts. They paused at each animal and drove their blades into an exposed area of neck, searching, as they twisted and pushed with the knives, for an artery or the beast's spine. Again and again the whales cried, adding to the terrible sounds in both water and air, until, suddenly, one voice would be lost as, at last, a blade found its mark and blood gushed and the whale threw its tail at the beach.

There was no order, in spite of the presence of a hunt sheriff and the foremen. Flensers were working in among the dead and dying, slashing away the hot flesh. An overpowering stench blanketed the killing bay and the tide ran red, already seeping a mile out to sea. The islanders not directly involved with the hunt had begun a traditional chain dance, a rhythmic chanting of hundreds of verses as they linked hands and circled a fire; a ritual for the women and the old. Young boys were encouraged to enter the water up to their waists and stab away ineffectively with their little knives at half-beached whales. They too laughed as blood oozed over their hands and the huge creatures writhed.

Four hours after the beginning of the killing it was finally time for the calves that had been left rolling confusedly about their bleeding parents. Many of them had gone unnoticed against the bigger targets of the adults. There were only a few cries to be heard now, the desolate calls of the young ones. Jumping across the backs of the dead, and the boats left adrift among the carnage, the spearsmen drove their weapons at the little whales. At last there were so few cries that no one noticed if there was a baby still alive out there among the black, torn shapes. Men panted as they gathered themselves for the long hours of flensing. There were a lot of whales in the kill; too much work to cut the meat from every one. Many would be towed back out to sea and dumped. The boys too were tired and played at their task, digging away with their knives, carving their names in whale flesh.

Only Poulsen now drove with his spear, as rhythmically as the chain dance singing, feeling at every blow that wonderful resistance as the blade cut through gristle and blubber, watching the blood trickling from open wounds. Jákup Poulsen was a happy man.


One hundred and eighty miles south by south-east of the Faroes banks *Hannah*, bearing her strange, hidden cargo, crashed her way through the gathering Atlantic swells. Neither man on board noticed the blue and silver Icelandair plane high above, heading in the same direction and overtaking them.


Bowman and Fitzgerald were talking quietly to one another as the American stared hungrily at one of the Icelandic stewardesses.

'She is undoubtedly *the* most beautiful creature I have seen in a month.'

'Keep your mind on being an innocuous tourist,' chided Bowman.

'I am acting in a perfectly normal fashion. Son, I swear that any man who didn't feast his eyes on that glorious shape was abnormal. You going to tell me you didn't notice?'

Bowman laughed. He had noticed the beautiful woman and she had made him think of Vicky, their last night together just before he sold the house in London. He thought of her as she had slept, lying there in the sodium-glow, arms upraised, breasts taut. And he had said goodbye. There was some madness in that, some masochism; but he knew it was something extremely powerful that had dragged him away.

The propellers hummed and the aeroplane rocked in sudden turbulence. They were but an hour's flight out from where their adventure would really begin, a whole new world of dangers more obvious than those presented by the British Home Office.

'You have made a serious mistake, Willoughby,' said the cold voice of Head of Section C, Commander Royce. 'You should have passed this over to me as soon as you considered it to be high priority.' The chagrined Assistant Head did not comment. It was not his fault that the information concerning the submarine had come in too late for Section to take any positive action. It was the fault of those blunderers in Scotland. They had not even bugged the cottage, even with priority clearance on the directives. Damn them. 'Now we have lost them, and,' Royce looked up from the file as he spoke and stared unemotionally at Willoughby, 'their machine. What do you suggest we do now? Do tell me.'

'Inform the Foreign Office, Sir? MI6? Bowman and Fitz-gerald have left Britain . . .'

Royce raised his voice and quelled his assistant to silence. 'Yes, I noticed that you had allowed them to leave. Shall we try, however, to use our brains before we panic and pass over the file. "Six" would not be very impressed with this little lot.' He gestured at the papers on the desk. 'Bowman and the American have flown, earlier this evening, for the Faroe Islands, a Danish protectorate. They will be there at this moment. They were seen to leave Glasgow airport, where they and their baggage were thoroughly searched. Now, would you care to re-examine this list of their possessions and tell me what you notice appears to be missing.' He half threw the Customs list at Willoughby.

'The submarine,' he paused, 'Sir.' He hated Royce.

'Precisely, Willoughby. In fact the most offensive items on this list appear to be fishing tackle. Hardly startling is it?' His tone became harsh. 'Where is the submarine?'

'I don't know, Sir.'

Royce sighed and rubbed his temples with his fine, bony fingers. 'Can we assume that the wretched machine has not gone with them? Bowman was known to have a meeting with

Heath-Morton of *World-Watch* a few weeks ago. One suggests, therefore, that the submarine was built for that organisation. Somehow, Bowman has managed to get it to Heath-Morton's men, right under our noses. Not their style, perhaps, a submarine; but there it is. Our problem now, Willoughby, thanks to the poor show of your men in Scotland, is to find where the machine is hidden, and what they plan to use it for.'

'What about Bowman and Fitzgerald?'

'Perhaps they are on holiday, taking a well-earned break after being hounded by the inefficient staff of C and E Sections, and having completed, I repeat Willoughby, completed, building their wretched machine. I think,' he said slowly, 'that we can forget those two for a while. It seems they have gone fishing, and have evaded our own little net. Concentrate on the submarine, Willoughby. Find it and we can tidy up this file. If we find definite foreign links then we can pass it over to 'Six'. Concentrate on *World-Watch* and Bowman's own Professor at King's College. Have your men thoroughly search Bowman's place. There just might be a few clues there. If nothing comes from those sources then try Bowman's girlfriend, the Chambers woman. Softly, softly, Willoughby; I don't want this business out of proportion, just because it has been messed up so far.'


They had passed through Customs and Passport Control at Vágar without being searched or unduly held-up. Already they were outside the little air terminal waiting for the bus that would take them to the ferry for Streymoy island and Tórshavn. The north-west wind was cold, after the humid warmth of Britain, and the two men pulled up the collars of their anoraks as they waited.

'After Glasgow,' said Fitzgerald, 'I had expected a rather more intense reception here. You would have thought these guys would have been informed of the suspicions the British authorities have on us, especially about the *Rozinante*.'

'I have my own suspicions that the British do not know enough. I don't think they know about Claus, or that the submarine is on its way here. Besides, George, maybe we're just very small fish that they've decided are not worth catching.' Despite his rationalisation of the situation, Bowman was relieved that they had arrived without incident. The weeks or months ahead would engage them with enough problems. He tried to erase Heath-Morton's warnings and the 'watchers' in Scotland from his memory.

# 13

Like a dictator among his subjects, the whaling ship towered above the little fishing boats in Tórshavn west arm. Down below, on the floating jetty, stood Bowman and Fitzgerald.

'This is the ship that Claus told us about,' said the Englishman.

'Big ugly brute, isn't it?' The two men looked at the extended bows where the harpoon cannon rested, thirty-five feet above the waterline. The platform reached back towards the rusting steel bow-deck where the enormous winches loomed above the cutaway gunwales, through which the big baleen whales would be hauled. The cliff-like hull was a patchwork of red iron oxide and black paint. Her name, *Stormur*, was painted in white beneath the high, curving prow. She looked dangerous and imposing, disproportionately large against the smaller boats moored around her. 'If this thing catches us,' intoned Fitzgerald, 'I reckon *Rozinante* would be in a little bit of trouble.' At that moment a strongly built man with dark hair but fair-skinned, Icelandic looks appeared on deck. He walked casually towards the bows and looked down on the two spectators. A cigarette hung from his mouth. He spoke in Faroese, slowly and with a slight, drunken drawl.

'You looking at my beautiful boat, eh? You look but not touch.' He threw the cigarette butt over the side. It spun down and narrowly missed Fitzgerald's head. The American stared up with an exaggerated smile.

'Steady, George,' whispered Bowman, 'there is no point in starting anything here.' Then he shouted up in English towards the figure on the deck. 'We were admiring your fine ship. I hope you don't mind.'

'Onglendingur, Ja?' Bowman nodded. The man continued in English. 'You look like conservationists. I do not let conservationist rats near my ship.' Bowman told him that they were boat-builders and were admiring the fishing vessels in Tórshavn, particularly the lean, fast lines of the *Stormur*.

'Very impressive. How fast can she go?'

'Fast. *Stormur* is the fastest ship in these waters.'

Bowman shook his head in mock astonishment. 'Would you allow us to see on deck?' The man stared at Bowman for a few moments, then at the smiling Fitzgerald.

'Ja, you come and see the deck of my fine ship.'

They stood on the flensing deck, aft of the cannon platform. Bowman looked towards the wheelhouse. 'May I look in there? I've never seen a whaler from inside.' The Faroese took an almost empty bottle of whisky from a pocket of his heavy coat. As he lifted the drink towards his lips he hesitated.

'You have some alcohol to give me? Some duty free perhaps?' Bowman said that he would try to find him a litre or two. 'Ja, I show you my wheelhouse.' He emptied the bottle and then threw it overboard. It smashed on the jetty and the man laughed. 'Poulsen is my name,' he announced as he took Bowman by the arm and led him off the flensing deck. Fitzgerald followed closely behind. 'I'm famous here; the best whaler in the North Atlantic, better than the Norwegians. You will hear of me. Everyone knows me here, even the Russian trawler men.' He continued to boast as they entered the wheelhouse where bottles and cigarette packets were strewn around the confusion of dirty machinery. Bowman was barely listening. Within less than a minute he knew how fast the *Stormur* could travel in a calm sea, the power of her diesel engine, the type and range of her radar and sonar apparatus. Suddenly Poulsen turned towards Fitzgerald. 'I kill a lot of whales, you see. I am a record holder. The Russians seek advice from me; the Norwegians and Icelanders follow me to the whales.'

'That's wonderful, congratulations.' The American's contempt was undisguised. The skin around his eyes was creased, but it was no longer a smile. He stared down at Poulsen, like a great eagle waiting to attack.

'You are American. I don't like you, American. I think you are a conservationist rat. I don't like you on my boat.'

Fitzgerald stopped smiling. He knew Bowman had learnt all he could. There was no further point in the pretence. 'I do not like you or your damn boat, Poulsen. You do not impress me in the least. Back home the kids fresh out of high school would be laughing at you.' The Faroese grabbed one of the empty bottles and lifted it towards the American. 'Before you allow me to do you some permanent damage, Son, I suggest you put that thing down.' Fitzgerald's attitude had become dangerous as he loomed over the motionless drunk. His big hands came up and clasped around the bottle. Poulsen stared and loosened his grip.

'You get off my boat, now, or I call my men, I call the Politi.' Fitzgerald smiled again. He dropped the bottle at Poulsen's feet where it smashed.

'You should not drop bottles overboard,' he said. 'Broken glass can hurt people and animals. I'm sure you wouldn't want that to happen, now would you?' Then he turned and left the wheelhouse, followed by Bowman. As they reached the jetty, Poulsen shouted from the whaler's decks.

'You do not come back here, conservationist rats. You leave Tórshavn; leave Føroyar. My friends come and get you otherwise; *my* men.'

'You know any *real* men, Poulsen? Maybe you got some on board that penile extension you call a boat, huh,' Fitzgerald shouted in return. He laughed and he and Bowman walked away from the gesticulating figure on *Stormur*'s decks.

'You can be a mean bastard, George.'

'Only when I have to be, Son.' Then his tone changed. 'That meat-head is not all hot air. He's going to be very dangerous. You see his eyes when I dropped the bottle; hell, there's a madman behind those eyes. I don't think he likes me very much.'

'I think you're right about that.'

Jákup Poulsen found it easy to hate, as easy as he found it impossible to love. Passion was easy; cruel, long passion; the way he hurt the Faroese girls, the way he shot finbacks with cold harpoons, rather than grenade heads, just to prolong the pain and the struggle. It was fun even to plan his passions, to run the cannon sights slowly over a cow-whale's back, or to tie the girls up before he started to hurt them; and now to look at the big American walking away from the jetty and to plan how he would get him one night soon, hoping that he would stay in Tórshavn. Already he could imagine how it would be as the whaling men held the big man kneeling on the ground, as Poulsen kicked him, and maybe used the knife on him; one slash across the face for every insult. They would get him, Poulsen thought, and the Englishman.

On the ferry across to Suduroy, the south island, Bowman and Fitzgerald stayed out on deck. The sea was calm as the ship skirted Sandoy. In the brilliant sunshine the brightly painted houses of Skálavík stood out garishly against the muted greens, browns and greys of the islands, but were subdued by the opalescent blues of the ocean.

Both men watched as the ship slid past the beautiful islands, and both shared the same thoughts; that the idyllic vista out there hid a devastating scar on the Faroese lifestyle.

The whaling had been a subsistence activity once, like the fishing, sealing and fowling; but not any more, except for the fishing. You could have understood it then, thirty years ago, when a few hundred whales a season were killed to supply meat for the long, dark winters, when not a scrap of meat was knowingly wasted, when even the bones were smashed and laid out to fertilise the land. You could see the need. Now, with several thousand pilots, and no one knew how many finbacks, slaughtered each year, and the terrible, wanton waste, and the money pouring in from Denmark so that there were no poor people on the islands any more, you could see it for what it had become: a sport.

# 14

Two miles off the east coast of Sandoy the *Hannah* rolled on the easy groundswell. Jens Petersen held her at slow speed while he and the other three men talked.

'Two days ago,' said Claus, 'was the first *grind* of the year. Three hundred whales were killed at Miðvágur on Vagar. I think there will be some more kills soon; Jens and I have seen two separate schools of *grindvhal*, one north-west of Streymoy, the other among the outer islands to the north-east.'

'We need to get some recordings of both schools. Can we get among them, preferably with the sub?' asked Fitzgerald.

'No problem approaching them in *Hannah*; but to do so unobserved is going to be difficult,' replied the tall Dane.

'It probably doesn't matter if this boat is seen once or twice,' said Bowman. 'You have your fishing licence to work within the three-mile limit. It is *Rozinante* that must not be seen.'

'Ja, but if Poulsen sees us there will be trouble, licence or not; and if there are whales around, Poulsen will find them as fast as we can.'

Fitzgerald shrugged. 'What can the bastard do if we are there, among his precious targets. We . . .'

'You do not understand Jákup Poulsen,' interrupted Claus. 'He is, without doubt, the most dangerous man in these islands. He is quite insane and he will seek trouble by any means. The law means nothing to him. And I might remind you that we also will be breaking the law. We are doing so now simply by having that machine of yours on board. None of us can consider taking protection in the law. Jákup has the will, and certainly the means, with *Stormur*, of destroying us. Our only hope is secrecy and cunning.' The men were silent for a while as *Hannah* stole across the sea, the rhythmic thudding of her engine sounding peculiarly loud to them all, exposing them to anyone who might be watching or listening on the nearby island. It was Jens who spoke first.

'You should tell them, Claus, the other reason why Jákup is so strong, and such a danger to us; tell them about Eidi.'

'Ja, the complication, the twist in the tail,' Claus smiled sardonically; 'my Eidi.' And he told them about the woman he loved, Poulsen's sister, and perhaps the one slightly stabilising influence on the whaler's life. 'I cannot stop him, for to do so I would have to kill him. I cannot do that; he is Eidi's blood and she loves him because he is the only one left of her family. He knows I love her, but has forbidden her to see me. We meet in secrecy, always in secrecy. He knows he can control me, while he has her.'

'Damn, Son, can't you just grab her and take her away?'

'You must try to understand. The situation here is not like anything that could happen in America, or Britain. This is an outland,' he nodded towards the rugged, lonely coastline. 'People here are closer to the old ways. Eidi could never leave Jákup on Føroyar. She believes the evil within him would consume him, and then her in punishment for her desertion. She is right, I think.'

'As you say,' interjected Bowman, 'we must, therefore, work in secrecy. If Poulsen appears on the scene, we must not confront him.'

Claus laughed bitterly. 'Jákup will confront us, do not deceive yourselves. We must work quickly, before he becomes too hungry for more killing, or before the whales approach too closely to another whaling beach. Cunning and speed; come, Jens, full speed for the northern fjords. We go and tape the whales' music, ja?'


That night, in a mild westerly wind, four miles north of the outer islands, they found their first school of pilot whales. It had

92

been sudden, as always with the *grindvhal*; an untroubled surface, then whoosh, whoosh, as ten black backs rolled and ten whales blew, then another ten, and *Hannah* was surrounded.

For several minutes the men watched, unable to do anything but marvel at the sight of the great beasts wallowing on the surface. The boat crept ahead, the sound of her engine subdued against the roar of whale breath and the sloshing of waves on their broad backs. Then Jens was working the winch and lifting the assembled submarine over the side.

'They're not frightened,' marvelled Bowman.

'They are never concerned by the fishing boats so far off-shore,' said Claus. 'Only in-shore, when the fishermen make a lot of noise, do the *grindvhal* become frightened; but even out here, with just the *Hannah*, they will not stay for long, four or five minutes perhaps, no more.'

There were no boats in view. They had noticed a Soviet trawler off the northern tip of Kalsoy, but this, now, was lost to sight against the shouldering expanse of the islands to the south.

'We will need about two hours,' said Bowman as he and Fitzgerald climbed aboard the *Rozinante*. 'Allow *Hannah* to drift unless the school gets more than half a mile away; in which case follow it. Try not to use the engine too much, because the noise will interfere with George's recording. We will be able to find you on our sonar if you are within a mile, maybe more. If other boats come too close warn us by approaching the school at full speed and by leaving your depth sounder on. If you cannot pick us up without being observed then get out. We can make it to the coast and the hiding place if necessary.' With that he nodded to Jens to release the winch ropes and he sat down next to Fitzgerald in the cramped cabin. 'Everything working, George?'

'Perfect, Son, just perfect.' They pulled down the hatch as they drifted away from the trawler. Bowman started the motors and steered the boat out towards the pilot whales. He examined the information on the screen. With an abrupt feeling of trepidation he noticed the depth reading of 480 feet. That was a lot of black water below them, he thought. The *Rozinante* would be crushed if she fell much more than a quarter of that depth. It would be a death that most submariners contemplated only in their nightmares; but sudden, just a second or two as the hull gave out and the water blasted all sense away.

The moments before a dive always made him think about the finality of a ruptured hull at depth. He struggled to blank the image from his mind. He concentrated on the screen, felt the reassuring vibration as the electric motors hummed and drove them along the surface. The boat yawed on the swell.

'O.K. George, here we go; let's get below.' He opened the ballast valve and the machine began to lose headway as she dropped lower in the surface. Bowman could sense his friend's tension. 'She's fine George, behaving just as she should.' Then the *Rozinante* was submerged and already less affected by surface movements. Bowman allowed her to drop to twenty feet where she glided with virtually no up and down motion. There was a violent hiss as he opened the air lead which would supply positive ballast and hold them at that depth. In the weak light within the cabin Bowman saw the American's hands bunched tightly into fists. The boat's panels creaked and then there was almost silence, just the hum of the motors. Bowman reached out and clasped his friend on the shoulder. 'It really is fine, George. Now let's find these whales.'

The screen was a blur of objects as the *Rozinante* moved among the great mammals, and the noise of their chatter filled the cabin – a whiplash of echo-location signals as the animals examined the strange craft in their midst. Bowman cut the motors. Through the viewing windows they could see the slight shimmer of the surface above them. Against that light hung dark shapes, ghosts stealing in and out of the blacker depths, into the blue haze above. The men were silent, totally overawed by the fantastic sounds and the huge, elusive shapes wafting past. A whale's fin brushed gently near the hull and a current slightly tilted the submarine. Close off to port both men saw a whale hanging motionless in the sea, obscuring all light.

The leader whale and the boat hung in the deep, and the babble of voices was steadily diminishing. Very slowly the massive animal rose to the surface and the two men could see the bulbous dome of its head and the long foreflippers, then the great, grey belly tapering down to the wide tail shrugging at the sea. Bowman adjusted the motors so that they were turning feebly and the *Rozinante* followed the pilot. Again a sound engulfed the boat, a vibration more powerful than that produced by the motors.

'He's talking to us,' explained Fitzgerald, his voice unsteady. 'Or examining us. His sonar can tell him far more than his eyes.' Bowman's skin was tingling as the sound seemed to grip him and pull at his flesh, to resonate within the boat's hull. Abruptly it ceased and the leader had disappeared, merging with the other shapes. 'Apparently he doesn't mind us being here.'

'There are a lot of whales below us now,' said Bowman as he examined the signals on the screen. 'They're diving.'

'Feeding, on squid; maybe two or three hundred feet down, maybe on the bed. They take it in turns. Ten or twenty all diving together, leaving the rest of the school up here. Hell, they're noisy.' The American was beginning to enjoy himself. 'Some whales hardly make a sound, like blues and finbacks. You have to record the very low frequencies to hear anything at all. These, and humpbacks and orcas, are the best of all; but I shouldn't think many people have heard them like this, right in among a feeding pod.'

Bowman had rarely seen the American in such an ebullient mood, he thought detachedly. Fitzgerald was obviously excited, but there was more, beyond excitement, as his fingers rapidly adjusted the recording apparatus. His eyes were open so wide as he stared out of the viewing ports for glimpses of the whales. You can know someone well, and yet you see a new person if you put him in a position in which he can almost touch an animal as big and intelligent as the *grindvhal* – when the man is relatively powerless and vulnerable; when the whale is master.

The school was travelling slowly east, not yet ready for the migration across the northern ocean to the Iceland banks. This was a small group, only seventy animals, some young, some very old, the result of a natural split in one of the larger schools that had collected in Faroese waters. There were several pregnant females among them and they would not travel open ocean until their calves were born.

The cabin escape valve hissed as stale air was released to the sea and fresh air was pumped in from the tanks. The *Rozinante* had been running for over an hour, quietly cruising behind the main body of the school. She had used little energy from her substantial battery.

'Have you recorded enough?' inquired Bowman. 'Shall we see if the system works?'

Fitzgerald hesitated as he reminded himself of the ultimate reason why he and the Englishman were diving with the whales. 'I guess we had better try it out.' He was apprehensive. Sonar responses had been the only way that researchers in the Caribbean had managed to attract humpbacks from any distance. Pilots, with their extraordinarily highly developed echo-location, should be more responsive to recorded sound; but it had only been tried in tanks.

Bowman checked the *Hannah*'s position, half a mile behind the school. The submarine was lying at a depth of twenty-two feet with over five hundred feet below her. There was a blur of signals on the screen which were the whales up ahead. *Rozinante*'s sonar could not penetrate that wall of animal flesh. With the machine switched to passive, only to receive relatively intense sound sources, there was again only a blurred fuzz on the upper part of the screen, the pilot whales, and no apparent propeller noises. Even the *Hannah*'s signal had disappeared. Bowman had no other way of telling if there were any vessels in the water beyond the school, although he knew that Claus would let him know of any impending danger. He switched the sonar back to active and increased the motor speed.

At just under three knots the boat hummed her passage through the school. Now she was in shadow as four whales rolled above them on the surface, then again in light. A big female lay up ahead at the same depth as the submarine. The two men caught a brief glimpse of a much smaller shape close by the whale's side, a young calf. The five-foot long animal, a perfect miniature of its mother, was suddenly aware of the approaching machine. In a moment, a flick of its flukes and twist of its foreflippers, it had rolled over the female's back and hidden on her far side. She lofted her wide tail and also turned away, her calf completely hidden now and protected by her deep flank.

The school swam aft of the submarine. Fitzgerald switched on the transmitter and adjusted its volume until they could hear quite clearly the recorded chatter of the whales with the occasional growl of the leader pilot. Again Bowman switched the sonar apparatus briefly to passive. The screen was empty, utterly devoid of signals. *Rozinante* was the only noise source in the sea. The whales were listening.

Easing the submarine to port, Bowman set course for due north, away from the islands. Fitzgerald slightly increased the transmitting volume. The leader whale's growl again resonated through the hull.

On the screen the whale school appeared to be falling away behind, as if poised, deciding between continuing east or turning north. Then Bowman and Fitzgerald watched as the blur began to close on the screen's centre. Soon there were shapes again dancing past the viewing windows, and chatter and growling and buffeting currents as whales spun close to the hull. Both men laughed and Fitzgerald slapped his friend on the shoulder. 'It works, Son. We two are a pair of geniuses.'

Bowman increased the boat's speed towards its maximum. The motors vibrated dangerously as they rapidly consumed the batteries' charge. Fitzgerald had the transmitter's volume also close to full power. At over six knots, with the Drift carrying her, *Rozinante* swept due north. Seventy whales followed, seventy voices calling; seventy animals swimming away from the terrible dangers that waited among the islands.

Under power the boat dived deeper, creaking as the panels deformed under the increasing pressure. The transmitter was switched off as Bowman levelled the machine at fifty feet. Outside, at that depth, was almost total darkness. It was five o'clock in the morning and they had been away from the *Hannah* for three hours and had led the *grindvhal* a total of four kilometres farther off-shore. Now and then they had heard the trawler's propeller, but, otherwise, there had only been the whale song. The submarine's batteries were half discharged and Bowman knew they probably would not have enough power to travel all the way to shore, nearly ten kilometres, against the flow of the Drift, and certainly not submerged. The *Hannah*, however, was still there, following a kilometre or two to the south.

The whales had gone, disappearing against the enormous wastes of ocean. The ballast tanks were filling with air as *Rozinante* rose towards the surface, returning to the light. Among a chaos of bubbles and heavy swell she broached the seas a few hundred metres away from the trawler.

Within five minutes the submarine lay on the *Hannah*'s deck and the men were climbing out of the cabin.

'You have been away too long,' insisted Claus. 'Two hours, you said, and it has been nearly three and a half. We are very exposed out here. A boat passed by two or three kilometres away. We threw out nets in case they were suspicious. There are no fish out here, just squid. Bastards must think we're crazy fishermen.'

# 15

*Hannah* was moored at Vestmanna, a small village on the Streymoy side of the steeply walled Vestmannasund. It was two in the morning and yet the four men sat on deck, talking quietly. They were tired, for there had been little sleep during the past week as they had searched for the whale schools. They had found only three; the group of seventy animals north of the outer islands, another small pod west of Vágar and a larger school some ten kilometres off Sandoy. All the whales had been too far off-shore to be herded into any of the whaling bays and, so far, the islanders had left them alone.

Because of the perpetual light, and the fine, calm weather the visibility around the islands was excellent and the men on board *Hannah* had risked only two more dives in *Rozinante*. Fitzgerald had more than eight hours of recordings of the schools and Bowman now had a fair idea of the submarine's limits of performance. They were frustrated, however, by their lack of mobility. As soon as any one of the schools came too close in-shore, *Hannah* would have to be taken there immediately. If she was too late and the islanders had begun a *grind*, there would be no hope of preventing the entire school from being destroyed. And yet if they were there in time, Fitzgerald and his sound apparatus could produce various reactions from the whales, ranging from a following response to fear, which would drive the whales off-shore. By trailing a transmitter behind the *Hannah*, they had already drawn the large Sandoy school farther out to sea.

In the Faroes archipelago, however, there was a considerable length of coastline which could be approached at any time by a pilot whale school. On board the trawler they knew that they might not hear of a kill until it was over. Yet each man was determined that while they remained in the Faroes, until the season naturally brought an end to the hunting in August, there would not be a large-scale *grind*.

'The three schools we have found,' said Fitzgerald, 'are fairly far apart. Frankly I think we can forget about the whales north of the outer islands. I can't see them coming close to any place where they are likely to be hunted.'

'Klaksvík, maybe, on Borðoy,' interrupted Claus. 'It is a big community, the biggest in Føroyar after Tórshavn. There have been nearly as many *grinds* there over the past twenty years as at Miðvágur. Then there is Hvannasund, also on Borðoy; a good whaling fjord.' He shook his head as he thought of the possibilities. 'But I think you're right, those whales will soon be crossing to Iceland. Only if there is a bad north wind will they come back south, among the islands. If that happens, my friends, there will be a *grind* on Borðoy, unless we get there first. We must watch the weather.'

'The problem with those outer islands,' said Jens, 'is that the whales take shelter in enclosed waters during stormy weather. There are many storms here, and many whales are killed in those fjords.' He shrugged his shoulders. 'It is the way it is. My father used to live in the village at Haraldsund, in the times when they needed the whale meat to survive the winter. He lived there for six years before he came to Denmark where he met my mother. He used to tell me stories about the whaling. He said that when the summer was stormy the people knew that there would be plenty of whale meat for the winter. They really needed the whales in those days, you understand. Without them their children died of starvation or there was no oil for the lamps during the dark months. Now they have electricity, and money, and food from all over the world; but they do not forget the whaling. It is part of their history that they are not willing to forget. They still need it to satisfy their pride, their links with the past.'

Claus watched Bowman and Fitzgerald as Jens spoke. He

could see that they understood. 'Jens is right. That is the feeling all over these islands; but it is perhaps strongest in the outer group. They are closer to the past out there, and away from the relatively modern ways at Tórshavn. They remember the old subsistence whaling. They are good people, who have resisted change for the right reasons. On the main islands the people have gone along with change, or accepted it, and are being destroyed by it. Here they hunt the whales for sport rather than food. They hunt them also to annoy the foreign conservationists.'

'To annoy the conservationists? Why?' asked Fitzgerald.

'It is part of an evil game they play here, and a reaction to change,' explained Claus. 'Føroyar is a young nation, proud of its geography, its isolation. It depends now on money from Denmark in order that its people can live to the standard of other Scandinavians. That embarrasses them. They would far rather be totally self-sufficient, relying entirely on the fishing, sealing and whaling, as they once did; but that would not pay for the goods they want from Europe and America. So they react in a peculiar way towards other nations. Every year now they have conservationists coming here and telling them that the whaling is wrong and cruel. The Faroese are angry and stubborn, and they hate interference. They will tell an Englishman, say, that he should go home and sort out the terrible problems in his own country. They will mention the leaking nuclear reactors and acid rain and agricultural chemicals and they will laugh at you if you mention the *grind*, which to them is hardly a problem compared with the way the English, or other Europeans, are poisoning the seas. I understand their feelings. I am closer to them, their mentality. So I understand why they will kill many whales even as the conservationists watch.'

'And yet,' said Bowman, 'you are helping George and me.'

'Ja, but that is for other reasons. I do not see you as English or American, and certainly not as conservationists, but as individuals and my friends. I know that you are men who despise all bad things that happen, wherever they occur. If you had not come here, to Føroyar, you would have attacked something else that you see as evil. You came here; so Jens and I help you.'

101

'You said there were several reasons?' Fitzgerald prompted him.

'I love these islands, as Jens does. Neither of us wishes to see the *grind* become something by which other nations crucify this place. And we love the whales, as you do. We have seen too many of them destroyed unnecessarily. We have heard them cry too often, and we know that there is little time left. Here, on the main islands, because of Poulsen and his thoughtlessness, because of some of the conservationists and the damn journalists that come here and dig up the trouble, the killing has become a sport and a bloody mess. We will help you to put an end to all that.'

'You have no love for the conservationists,' suggested the American.

'For what is in their hearts, I have respect, just as I have for your beliefs. But I cannot watch the way they work without becoming angry. They make no attempt to understand the minds of the people. You have to understand the whole if you are to affect a part. They tell the Faroese that the *grind* is something from the past and is cruel and unnecessary today. That much is true. Even many of the Faroese believe that. But the conservationists ruin all their good work by distorting the truth. They describe to the rest of the world the killing that happens here out of context, without all the background that provides the complete picture, the truth. They create the illusion that every Faroese is like Jákup Poulsen. The conservationists are not bad, many might even be good; but I think most of them are misguided. But worse, far worse, are some of the journalists who come here. They are bad men, with their lies and the money they make out of the bloody stories. They need men like Poulsen for the best stories, and they pay people to do terrible things while the cameras catch it all on film. They incite and develop evil in the Faroese.'

'That's journalists the world over, Son; integrity is not their middle name,' intoned Fitzgerald.

'Ja, but they should not come here with their corrupt ways.' After a moment he continued. 'I am a smuggler. People would say that was wrong; but I never did anything that was as evil as some of those bastard journalists.'

Later that night Jens left the trawler while the three other men continued to talk. 'He is off to see his Christianna, or Asa or Josefina, I forget who it is in Vestmanna. He will get himself in trouble one day. The Faroese hate foreigners interfering with their womenfolk, even us Danes.'

'Will you see Eidi soon?' asked Bowman.

Claus looked at the Englishman, a sudden fear or sadness in his eyes. 'Ja, when next we are in Tórshavn I will see my Eidi.'

Fitzgerald had been mulling over the things about which Claus and Jens had talked. 'You know these people, Claus,' he said. 'Where do you think the next *grind* will be?'

'That will depend on the whales far more than the islanders. Wherever a school approaches land the cry will go up: "Grindaboð", and everyone will take to the boats and start herding the whales. In calm weather the *grindvhal* tend to be dispersed and hang a long way off-shore, as we have found. Most of the squid tend to be over deep water, so the *grindvhal* are there too. When the wind blows up, the good fishermen know where the schools will seek shelter. I know too; but we will have to wait for the wind.'

Vestmanna lay in shadow from the early morning sun. The men looked across the Sound towards Vágar where the cliffs and grassy hills were orange and golden above the inky blue of the sea. A few torn fragments of cloud hung around the summits of Jatnagardar and Reynsatindur, the sisters of stone, but the air was calm. A flock of terns rose above the shadow cast by the Streymoy cliffs, their wings a unified scarlet glow as the birds flew across the sea, searching for their first meal of the morning. Fulmars and oyster-catchers were also in the air, circling and gliding.

103

'You see why I love this place,' continued the Dane. 'The sea is so rich and the land so poor; but both are so beautiful, Ja? Together, I think, the islands and the ocean, and the weather too, make a very special place here. Only the men spoil it; we cannot live in balance.' He looked at his companions and smiled. 'Do not worry, my friends, you should get some sleep now. We will not miss anything, I promise. While the weather is calm the whales will be safe off-shore. There will be a time when you will need to be wide awake and when we must move quickly. The weather here is capricious. It will change soon; then I will know where to take *Hannah*.'

**16** Head on to a freshening south-easterly the *Hannah* rushed at full speed towards Suduroy, the long swell smothering her foredeck and growling along her hull. Visibility had diminished as rain clouds ushered in showers. The sun occasionally broke through and the south island then appeared incandescent as it bathed in the light, its green more lush than before, its rock faces glistening.

'The two best whaling bays on Suduroy,' shouted Claus above the sound of the racing engine and the noise of the trawler's passage through the sea, 'are called Trongisvágs-fjörður and Vágsfjörður. Many whales are killed there each year. They have not yet had a *grind* this season, which is unusual. They are usually the first. Now that the summer storms have arrived they will want a kill, before the schools all pass up to the main islands. There,' he pointed towards the island, 'beyond that headland they call Skarvatangi, Shag Point, is Trongisvágsfjörður. It is very narrow; once the whales go in there they never escape. We must stop them.'

The south-easterly, combined with a running tide, was lifting curtains of white water against the island's shores. 'There will be a school along this coast,' continued Claus as he turned the helm to meet another gushing sea; 'maybe more than one. These conditions push the squid in close, and the whales after them. This time of year, also, in weather like this, the females like to be near the fjords so that they can find protection from bad winds for their calves.' The Dane's blond hair streamed in the wind and it occurred to Bowman that he looked the part of the Viking raider as he shouted to make himself heard above the incessant roar, the wet skin of his face shining, his broad hands gripping the wheel.

Bowman felt thankful that he had the right men to do a job worth doing. He had never had the slightest doubt about Claus, or his able companion. He sensed something far more important than their physical power, than their reliability or courage. It was their will to do the job as well as it could possibly be done, and their belief in its purpose. Claus was looking at him.

'Well, mad bastard Englishman? We cannot see the whales in this big swell, but they are here, very close. It will be dangerous for you in your little boat, even to launch it will be dangerous. But if you do not go, the wind will fall tonight and there will be *grindvhal* off Trongisvágsfjörður. The villagers will not let them get back out to sea.' He turned to Fitzgerald as the American lifted his hands to the headphones he was wearing. 'You hear anything?'

'They're near. I keep getting bursts of sonar; not much, but definitely pilots.' He took off the headset and retrieved the hydrophone that had been trailing from the stern.

'Looks like we go right away,' said Bowman decisively. 'Anything we should know, Claus?'

'The ferry will be coming through here in about an hour, and another one, two hours later, going down to Vagsfjord. In this,' he nodded towards the pitching seas, 'there will be few fishing boats out until the wind falls. The current will be pushing you along, and in places it is very strong. If you are too close in-shore you could meet a violent backwash in these conditions, so be careful.'

In the comparative shelter of the wheelhouse Bowman and Fitzgerald studied the chart as Claus pointed out the areas where there were dangerous currents. 'We will set you adrift here. After you have dropped your noise device at the mouth of the fjord you will make your way up the coast to here.' He marked the place with the point of his knife. 'Meanwhile, Jens and I take *Hannah* down to the southern point of the island, here at Akraberg.'

106

'Then,' interrupted Fitzgerald, 'you drop the transmitter over the side and switch the volume to full while you make your way slowly back up the coast. I guess you'll scare every whale for hundreds of miles when they hear what's on that machine, but it's all for their well-being. With luck, they'll follow us around the top of this island and into the open sea. Just remember to turn the tape over every hour. If it jams, then rip it out and put in this spare.' He handed him the cassette.

'What is the noise you have on here?' asked the Dane.

'It's actually a recording of a pack of hunting killer whales I made in the Pacific a few years back. I reckon there's only one animal that pilot whales fear more than men, and that's the killer whale.'

Claus laughed. 'Ja, clever bastard; *mastravhalur* we call the killer whale. He frightens the *grindvhal*. He frightens the Faroese fishermen too. Ja, we will be a *mastravhalur*.'

'You'll be a whole damn pack of them.'


The vent valve hissed as *Rozinante* levelled at a depth of thirty feet. Even there she rose and fell slightly in the swell. It was mid-afternoon and the sea was well lit around the submarine. The men watched the silver shimmer of bubbles that rose from the valve towards the surface. Bowman examined the monitor.

'There's a strong current pushing us on-shore at this depth. We'll use it to get into the mouth of the fjord where we can drop your noise box. Then, maybe, we can use an undercurrent to push us back out.' He was enjoying himself. Submarines in the North Sea always worked in powerful currents around the rigs. He was used to such conditions, as much as anyone ever could be.

The motors hummed but there was a greater vibration than usual throughout the boat. Fitzgerald was tense as the violent tide pulled and pressed at the delicate glass-fibre. Bowman was detached, barely hearing the clawing waters or feeling the ominous shaking. He concentrated on the screen and his instruments. It was the only way he ever held himself from panic during a dive, by concentrating on the workings of the machine. It suppressed his imagination.

The mouth of the fjord was only two kilometres across. The submarine nudged close to the northern edge. The currents were increasingly more powerful close to the shore. Bowman rapidly worked at the rudder and changed the motor speeds until they were less than a hundred and fifty metres from the headland. *Rozinante* barely moved, and yet her motors whirred at almost full power, holding her against the enormous force of the backwash.

Bowman could not risk moving any closer to the growling surf and the teeth of rocks. He nodded to Fitzgerald.

The sound device, a simple underwater transmitter, powered by a heavy duty twelve-volt battery, fell to the sea floor. For the time being it was silent. Fitzgerald had set it on a time switch so that it would begin transmission later. It would continue to emit its sound, a steady shock of noise, for over a week until the battery was exhausted. Four devices had already been dropped in the shallow water near the mouths of the most frequently used whaling fjords of the central islands. While the devices continued to emit their signal, whales would not approach within several kilometres. It was Fitzgerald's idea to replace the machines every week. Thus they were forming a noise barrier around those places where the whales would be in greatest danger.

*Rozinante* tilted as she turned against the tide. At a depth of less than twenty feet she struggled with the currents. There was a constant rumble of noise and a great thudding as the seas hit the hull and slid over the boat's tapering body. Still the motors whined at full power and yet she barely moved. Bowman opened the ballast valve and, slowly, *Rozinante* dived towards the sea floor. Then, at thirty feet, with another twenty below her keel, she was poised.

'We must be above a reef,' shouted Bowman. 'There's an upwelling preventing us from diving any deeper. Hold on George, anything can happen . . .' There was a bang as the boat jolted savagely. For a moment Bowman closed his eyes, pulling his head down into his shoulders as he waited for the terrible blast of icy water. It did not come. The submarine rocked and turned her nose towards the sea floor. Almost instinctively Bowman opened the air line to the ballast tanks and wrenched at the diving plane lever. Wide-eyed now he stared into the mysteriously spinning sea. He eased the motors to half power.

Incredibly slowly the boat steadied and came to rest on an even keel at a depth of forty feet. She rose slightly, silently, and was again under control.

'That never really happened,' whispered Fitzgerald.

'We've sprung a leak,' murmured Bowman coldly. He was looking at the seal along the cabin's roof. A steady runnel of water poured along the seam. 'We must have hit the bottom, nose first. We're reinforced there, but the seals have suffered from the shock. We'll have to run up the coast very shallow. He looked at the screen and then at the chart. They were just north of the fjord's mouth, rising very slowly towards the surface and turning to face north-west, directly up the coast. Bowman ran the motors at a third speed as the current gripped the boat's stern and carried her. 'We're lucky the current's going our way. The batteries are already down to half charge after that little adventure.'

Fitzgerald was muttering quietly to himself as he switched on his sound apparatus. Now it was his turn to lose himself in his own particular job, time to put the awesome dangers from his mind as the strange whale song filled the cabin, calming, a peaceful repetition of soothing calls.

It was almost hypnotic. Bowman could feel himself relax, becoming sleepy. *Rozinante* was running at twenty feet, pitching gently in the groundswell. Both men stared ahead at the flickering silver and blues of the sea. Neither noticed the intermittent blip on the starboard side of the monitor screen. It faded, disappeared and then returned, closer to the centre.

Suddenly Fitzgerald turned to Bowman. 'I can hear screw noises.' They looked at the monitor, seeing the signal immediately, almost coincident with the central point.

For long, agonising moments the tanks flooded as the

109

submarine again tilted her nose at the distant sea bed. The propeller noises were now a roar and the men could also hear the growl of water on a great hull, drowning the sounds of their own electric motors. Above them swept an enormous, eclipsing shadow, closer, falling towards them.

The ferry ship staggered in the deep swells, crashing down into the troughs. The giant steel blade of her keel axed into the sea towards the puny, unseen vessel below. Feet above the *Rozinante* it hung. As if in a nightmare Bowman could see the black steel scythe rolling above him, in a deadly slow motion, and the roar had become so loud that no sound was differentiated, just an apocalyptic detonation, and the dreadful, consuming darkness. Beyond fear, he sat and waited for what surely would be an instantaneous death, as the boat was smashed like drift wood and their bodies were thrown down into the sea. He felt the submarine turn and spin, flung through the darkness by some gigantic hand. He could see the light again, but it appeared to be coming from below. There was cold water on his face, and still the roar in his ears.

He could not remember the realisation that they had escaped being hit. It was minutes, perhaps, before he convinced himself that the boat was still intact. There was a powerful ringing in his ears. It gradually subsided to be replaced by an unearthly silence, then the hiss of water being forced through the hull at high pressure. There was no apparent light outside, and only the red glow of the monitor screen inside. The motors had stopped and *Rozinante* was motionless. She was resting, slightly unevenly, on the sea floor.

Bowman switched on the cabin light.

'I can see again,' said a friendly, though trembling, voice.

'It was the ferry, George.'

'I thought it was a battleship. Did it hit us?'

'No, but we've hit the bottom again. We are lying just over a hundred feet down. I would never have dared bring the boat to this depth; but here she is.' A fine spray of water, being forced through the main seal, separated the two men. Everything in the cabin glistened. Bowman switched on the forward flood lamp so that they could see the environment into which they had inadvertently stumbled. What they saw was a devastatingly bare rock-scape, reaching out into the dark waters; a cold, heartless graveyard for the foolhardy. Bowman could see how lucky they had actually been. There were spikes and edges of rocks reaching up from the boulder-strewn floor. Had the submarine landed on one of those her hull would certainly have been ruptured. At that depth and pressure the entire framework would then have been torn to shreds.

The ballast tanks were filled with water. Bowman opened the air lines to maximum, relieved, at least, to hear the reassuring hiss of air. The boat did not move. Both men knew that they needed only one of the main tanks to be intact and they would be able to return to the surface, but as they listened to the precious air draining from the store tanks they watched the jagged, unmoving rocks beyond the windows. They said nothing, but shared the same terrible fears as they willed their machine to save them.

She creaked and juddered and, abruptly, settled on an even keel. Then, almost imperceptibly at first, she was rising above the rocks. Bowman closed his eyes and released a long sigh. He closed the air line to a gentle flow as he watched the screen and the numbers which told him the depth. Less than a hundred feet now; ninety . . . He switched off the flood lamp and stared out into the darkness, waiting for that lovely first sight of natural light, the incredible dull blue haze you see when coming up from the black depths.

The veil of spray had subsided and the leak was again a runnel along the seam. Bowman was aware of his own uncontrollable trembling. He looked at Fitzgerald, who reached out and gripped his shoulder. 'Thanks, Son; that was probably the worst experience of my whole life.' Then they laughed, a hysterical, childish laugh; but one of utter joy.

# 17

Willoughby was smug. He had fitted together the pieces of the jigsaw until he had formed the complete picture, or what the new boys in C Section referred to as a 'situation of maximum probability'. The Danish trawler *Hannah* had been the missing link. Willoughby had spent several days hunting for the presence of just such a vessel through the Customs reports for northern Scotland. An official at Thurso had had his suspicions about the trawler's crew and had reported that a detailed 'sniffer' search had revealed no presence of drugs; but, as Willoughby knew, they had been examining for the wrong sort of smuggling. *Hannah*'s presence coincided with the disappearance of the submarine. Customs could not be blamed; they had no reason to suppose that the Danes would be smuggling something out of the country, and they hardly had the ships to police that coast adequately.

Royce read the report. 'You have done well, Willoughby; made amends for your earlier mishandling of this affair.' He stared coldly at the fat man sitting opposite him. 'I think you may have made the right supposition. Whaling, eh?' He lifted his eyebrows as if to air his surprise. 'Hardly seems worth it, does it, these fellows putting in all this effort just to interfere with a bit of local whaling?' Willoughby made no comment. It was typical of Royce to belittle something on which Willoughby had worked. 'You are sure, I suppose,' continued the gaunt Head of Section, 'that the trawler has made her way to the Faroe Islands?'

'Interpol are confirming that now, Sir.'

112

'Hm, well we shall find out shortly.' Again he studied the report. 'You did not find out very much from Victoria Chambers, Bowman's girlfriend, or the Professor.'

'Partridge is an acknowledged expert on, among other things, marine acoustic apparatus and guidance systems. It is reasonable to suspect that he built something for the submarine, or gave some advice on its construction. We have no proof, as yet. The Chambers woman is living in his Sussex home and has been doing so ever since Bowman left the country.'

'And I see that Fitzgerald has made rather a lot of money in the recording business and one or two other little ventures. Bit of an entrepreneur, our American.'

'He spends the money too; boats, marine parks, "save the whale" campaigns, anti-nuclear groups. Oh, and he's reputed to be a bit of an electronics nut.'

'All the right ingredients, as they say.' Royce half-closed his eyes, as if bored. 'All right, inform "Six", recommending they pass the information over to the Danish authorities. Usual procedure.' He waved a hand to dismiss his assistant.

'Er, I would like to work with the Foreign Office on this one, if I may, Sir. After all, there is an Englishman involved, so it's still our department.'

Royce hesitated and thought of refusing his permission, but he too was intrigued by this peculiar case. 'As you wish, for the time being.'


In calm conditions the trawler lay adrift north of Suduroy. She rocked gently on the storm's after-swell. The four men all looked towards the west where the spouts of whales could still be seen; rising, pink and orange against the low evening sun, suspended as vaporous plumes and then falling seaward. Even as they disappeared another group gushed into the sky.

'How many, Claus?' asked Fitzgerald.

'It is a very big school; biggest we have seen for a number of years. Eight hundred, possibly a thousand; it may even be more than one school. Perhaps several followed you round the northern point and joined here. Now they travel together. *Grindvhal* are very social, Ja?' He looked at Fitzgerald with something approaching admiration, which was rare for the Danish smuggler. 'You are clever, American. Your sound machines work well. You speak to the whales and they do what you ask.'

'Just so long as we keep them off-shore, Son; away from the whaling fjords.'

Bowman sat down heavily on a deck winch. He was suddenly tired as the realisation of what had nearly happened back in Suduroyarfjord turned into shock. He could not expel from his mind the vision of those rocks on the sea bed, more than a hundred feet down in the icy, high-pressure darkness, or the black blade of the ferry ship's keel hanging above his head, poised to crush him with a titanic blow. He trembled as he remembered the way the boat had dived so fast away from the light, uncontrollably, as she exchanged the danger on the surface for the unknown horrors below; and those moments she had not moved as he opened the ballast line. She had sat on the bed for what had seemed impossibly too long while the overpowering fear that the ballast tanks had been ruptured drove him towards panic; he felt again the cold spray from the seal leak on his face, and the incredible, pounding heat of blood surging in his head. He knew how close they had been to the end, that they had escaped by the most extraordinary good fortune. He knew also that they would have to use *Rozinante* again, several times, on every occasion that they needed to exchange Fitzgerald's sound emitters at the mouths of the whaling fjords, and every time they found a *grindvhal* school.

He was losing his nerve.

That was inexcusable. He looked up at the Danes and Fitzgerald as they watched the distant whales. It was he who had insisted on having good men to do the job, *really* good men? Yet now he felt a weakness within himself. He thought of his old job, the safe dives in the North Sea, the continual testing of machinery. It was all so tame compared with the thrill of taking *Rozinante* down into those dangerous in-shore waters.

114

He remembered the meeting with Hopkins, the North Fire executive; the way the bastard had tried to make him feel guilty. Vicky had attempted to warn him of the hidden dangers. But no one and nothing had stopped him, not Heath-Morton of *World-Watch*, not the British Secret Service, not the enormous difficulties. Now, however, he felt his courage wavering and he knew that once that faltered you were exposed, vulnerable to all fears and dangers. Once you turned your back on them and tried to run, they fed on you, until they had devoured you. He felt a trickle of sweat running down his temple.

Fitzgerald appeared to be so sure, unflustered by the disaster he had so narrowly escaped. He was still watching the whales as they swam farther and farther off-shore. Was his belief so much more intense than Bowman's, or was his courage so much stronger? How was it that his mind had apparently recovered from the terror they had both experienced during the last dive? Fitzgerald turned towards Bowman. In a moment he had interpreted the drawn expression on his friend's face.

'You look as tired as I feel. I reckon that you and I can get some sleep while these crazy Danes take us back to port.' He helped the unprotesting Englishman to his feet and led him below, nodding to Claus as they went.

Later, as Bowman and Fitzgerald slept, *Hannah* crept peacefully towards Tórshavn through the twilight of the small hours. Claus and Jens spoke in the wheelhouse.

'They are special men, our friends below,' said Jens. 'We would not go in their machine, under the waves. That is where only dead men go. And yet I have never known two men so alive as those. They do it for our whales, Claus.'

'Ja, and they also do it for themselves, to satisfy their conscience. They are clever also. They have made those whales off Suduroy safer, for a while, and we are the only men who know how they did it.' He laughed at the thought of the islanders who would be mystified as to where the *grindvhal* had gone, their anger at having lost a season's sport. Then he began to think about the task ahead of him and his companions. The great schools of whales would collect around the main islands

115

now, and there were many killing bays up there; Midvágur, Tórshavn, Vestmanna, Sörvágur, Kvívík, Götavick and more, where the whales could be slaughtered. So far he and his companions had only laid sound emitters in the most popular whaling areas. There was so much left to do. If only they had more than *Hannah* and the little submarine. If only there were other men like Bowman and Fitzgerald.

In the late morning the Danish trawler put in to Tórshavn harbour. After the previous day's gale, the strong sunlight was dazzling on the brightly painted buildings which reached high towards the Streymoy hills. The reds, blues and emerald greens, and the grass greens of the turf roofs contrasted with the landscape beyond, just as the beautifully coloured Faroese fishing boats, with their distinctive long-ship design, contrasted with the cold blue of the sea.

Few people gave the trawler a second glance, but Jákup Poulsen had seen her since she had rounded the long eastern quay. He had been watching from *Stormur*'s bridge. He lifted a whisky bottle to his lips as he smiled in satisfaction. It was time for some more sport.

A woman watched *Hannah* as she settled in the crowded harbour. Eidi Poulsen also was smiling, but there was no evil in her mind.

**18** 'They are hungry for more killing,' said Claus as he and Jens returned to the trawler with provisions. 'There has not been a *grind* anywhere on the islands since the kill at Miðvágur before we arrived. The young men are keen to be among the *grindvhal*. They are bored and drink too much and they have few outlets for their aggressions.' Around the harbour could be seen several groups of men, hands in pockets or clasping bottles of the local light beer, walking lethargically around the quaysides. It was late evening, the time when the little town came alive, as with all high-northern towns when the summer nights have no darkness; but Tórshavn was like no other place on earth.

Essentially Scandinavian, its clean streets wound among the wooden houses that crowded down towards the harbour. Here was the heart of the town, where the liners, ferries, fishing boats, whalers and freighters, came and went, where human life in the Faroe Islands was focused. It was a gathering place for men who worked the North Atlantic and its character was made up of every one of them; of the wild Greenlanders and the open, honest Icelanders; the Danes, Norwegians and Swedes; the strange Finns and a few, skulking in the quieter cafés in the town, who could only be Russian. Among them all were the native Faroese, descendants of Irish, Icelandic and Viking settlers. As Claus said, so many of them drank too much of the hard spirits smuggled off the numerous ships, and too many of them were bored.

Incongruous against the backdrop of traditional buildings was a Trans Am car, then a big Mercedes leading a stream of powerful cars along the barely adequate roads of the town.

117

'There, you can see their boredom,' explained Claus. 'They drive around the town, doing a little circuit. They can afford their expensive cars, even though they have no real use for them. So they drive around Tórshavn, trying to impress the young girls.' He looked at Fitzgerald and laughed. 'You wish you were that young again, my friend?'

'Just so long as I could know what I know now. I'd have a lot of fun.'

Claus laughed again and then was serious. 'Jens and I will be leaving you on board for a few hours tonight. You watch my boat, Ja?'

'You are a horny Dane.'

Claus smiled. 'Jens is, as you say, a horny Dane; but I am in love with just one woman, just one in the whole world.' There was neither pride nor flippancy in what he said. 'Maybe I will see her tonight, if Jákup becomes drunk enough. Maybe I simply get a message to her. We can never tell.'

'You need to take some positive action with that girl of yours.'

'It will happen soon. This summer, while we are here; something is going to happen that will end this game we play.'


During the small hours of that night it began. Bowman and Fitzgerald were on deck, while the Danes had been gone since midnight.

'Do you see what's coming along?' Fitzgerald nodded towards a group of men approaching the moored trawler. Leading them was Jákup Poulsen. He stared up at the men standing on *Hannah*'s deck.

'Ah, American rat, so you are on my friend Claus's boat. I knew you and I would meet again. It is only right that you are with Claus.' He looked towards Bowman. 'And you, Englishman, you too are a conservationist rat? You try to save the whales maybe?' One of the men behind him, the mad Icelandic engineer, let out a strange, half-choked laugh. 'Ja, Steini, the bastards here save the whales I think; good joke.' Fitzgerald and Bowman watched the group of men without expression. 'You go and fetch Claus now, American, I want to speak with him.'

'I'm so terribly sorry, Mr Poulsen, but Mr Hansen is asleep,' announced Fitzgerald. 'And so, I'm afraid, is Mr Petersen. Been fishing, you see; very tiring. They asked not to be disturbed. Can I take a message?'

Poulsen's face was drawn taut and his eyes betrayed his anger. 'You make a mistake when you annoy me, American. You treat me without respect. You think we joke all the time, huh?' The engineer was brandishing a knife and his eyes were wide. 'Na, na, Steini, we cut him up another day. I let you loose on him soon. See, conservationist rats, my men do not like you. They think you are bad, interfering foreigners. I think so too. You are in trouble if I do not like you.' He shook his head in mock sorrow. 'Claus is a silly man, looking after conservationist rats. He is getting soft now, eh? You can give him a message. You tell him that Jákup is going whaling tomorrow. Tell him I am after my finbacks and that I have twenty harpoons on *Stormur* and that every one of them is going to be put in a whale's back, or maybe I use one or two to sink this rubbish boat. You tell him that, American.'

'I will pass along your kind words.'


In the darkened room Claus and Eidi held one another, at peace for a while after their months of waiting.

'He is becoming more dangerous all the time.' She spoke quietly and yet Claus could hear the urgency in her voice. 'He speaks of an American and an Englishman who have annoyed him. He thinks they are conservationists and he wants to get at them. Are they with you?' Her fingers stroked down the Dane's rough chin and over his lips. She could feel that he was smiling.

'They are with me. Good men, the best I know; already they are protecting the *grindvhal*.'

'There is talk around the islands that there are few *grindvhal*

119

this year. They have not yet been seen off Suduroy or Sandoy. I think perhaps that is because your friends are good at what they do?'

'They are clever, Eidi, and they have courage.'

'Jákup also is clever. He knows you are not smuggling this time, and that you are here for something else.' She rose until she was sitting on the bed. Claus could see the dim light from the oil lamp reflected from her pale back, and her fair hair on her shoulders, her face half-turned towards him. 'He leaves tomorrow to hunt for finbacks. He is very excited about that.'

Claus closed his eyes. It was so early, he thought, for Jákup to be going after the finbacks. The Faroese were officially allowed only five of that species a year. Jákup was probably selling the whale carcasses on the high seas to Norwegians or Russians. He would do that.

'It will all be over soon, Eidi. It has gone on far too long already. I have to stop him.'

She rolled over until she was on top of him. 'How can you do that? He has too many men behind him and *Stormur* is so fast. You do not even have the Politi as he does. They will never side with you, a Dane; still less your English and American friends.'

'Still, it shall be done.'

'You will hurt him?'

'He is out of control, Eidi; he and his crew on *Stormur*.'

As she made to speak again he kissed her, quelling her doubts and her fears. The times they had together were too rare to be wasted talking about Jákup.

# 19

Spray smashed at his face and the cold wind stung his eyes as he stared towards the grey-blue shapes in the sea. Jákup Poulsen turned quickly to signal the helm dead ahead and then again looked towards where the massive animals had blown. He and a crew member stripped the covers from the cannon. Two more men were hurrying to the gun platform with a grenade-headed harpoon. From a long way off came the distinctive *whoosh* of a big finback spouting, and another soon after the first. Poulsen watched the towering plumes as they hung above the pitching waters. He signalled to port and almost immediately felt *Stormur* ease into the bulging seas.

Then he signalled to the helmsman to drop engine speed. The whales were running fast, across *Stormur*'s bow. If she approached on her present course Jákup would have to take a fast shot at the whale's flanks. He hated being too fast on a whale. It was untidy. This way, allowing the two beasts to run a mile or more upwind, he could chase them from behind. Soon the shapes were lost in the turbulence, even their spouts no more significant than the wave crests on the torn sea.

They were twenty miles east of Faroes, driving at a Force six from the north – an icy wind that brought a stabbing sinus pain. Poulsen ignored the intense aching. The first finbacks of the season had been sighted; pain did not matter when there was the thrill of chasing these big baleen whales. They were so fast, blasting their seventy tons along the surface. The more you frightened them the faster they swam. Sometimes they changed direction, or turned completely around and sounded beneath the boat. Until they got tired; then they wallowed and shot their hot breaths at the sky and, though you could not hear their subsonic cries, and the screams as the harpoons hit, you knew they were suffering.

*Stormur* was rushing again at dead ahead, half a mile behind the high blows. Poulsen swivelled the cannon up and down and from side to side, enjoying its satisfying, well-loved weight. He stared along the sights and felt the cold metal on his face. It had to hurt; to be best of all there had to be a little pain, to lift you, like a drug.

Then he smelt them, the heavy oiliness of their breaths, the smell that made young whalers sick, but which to the old hands was, again, a drug. They were only a hundred metres away now and he was beginning to distinguish their shapes. He saw a tail, blasting hard at the surface. The beasts were working hard; that was good, they were scared. Soon they would start to panic and would uselessly burn up all their energy. Poulsen laughed as he thought of their stupidity. With their power they were easily capable of out-manoeuvring even a vessel as fast as *Stormur*. They could dive for more than half an hour so that no one would see them on a wild sea. And yet they chose to run on the surface, giving themselves to the sport of the chase. They all did that, the sei, minke, even the blues. Only sperms and *mastravhalur* sometimes gave you problems. You could harpoon them ten miles from where they were first sighted, and several hours later.

The finbacks continued running into the wind. They could hear *Stormur*'s vibrating engines and the whirring propeller biting at the water, and the rhythmic crash of the swell on her pointed bows. Their great hearts were racing, but still they dashed away from the frightening noises. Now their tail flukes broached on each upsweep and they were losing control.

Poulsen had the larger of the two beneath the cannon. The metal extension dug into his armpit as he pressed his weight against it, lifting the sights. The grey mass out there was like a surfacing submarine, a curved bow-wave streaming off its back. The whale blew again, a hurried expulsion and gasp, running as it turned in the swell. The sights ran along the creature's back, on towards the wide head. Poulsen gripped the twist trigger. The animal's tail would be almost beneath *Stormur*'s bows now. He could see scars on the skin, testimony of old encounters with rocks, parasites and enemies in the sea. His right hand twisted.

The lovely gush of blue smoke, the heavy, ear-numbing bang, the massive harpoon flying, and the tether arcing, were glorious to Jákup Poulsen; like the wonderful, rushing waves during the pursuit as the whaler's engines ran hot, and the incredible scarlet mushroom that welled in the sea beneath the cannon platform.

The giant animal arched his long back as the grenade blew a metre deep in his blubber, and he lifted his head up at the sky. He hung there, blood pluming and pouring from the hole in his back. He thrashed at the waves as the overwhelming pain shot through his body and he screamed his terrible screams across the ocean. The tether from the harpoon tightened as the winches pulled, cutting the barbs into his belly. His seventy tons sagged and his tail wafted uselessly. He spun, wrapping himself in the ropes. He was deaf and blind to everything . . . but the pain.

Poulsen watched without blinking. His own heart was racing with the thrill of it all. He preferred cold harpoons, the type that did not explode within their target, so the whale would run with the spear in his back, towing the boat as the animal bled and poured out its energy; but hot harpoons were faster. This time Poulsen needed a quick kill. Behind him, his crew were reloading the cannon and attaching a fresh tether. The men did not watch the titanic struggles in the sea. It had been enough to feel the great thud as the harpoon flew. In such rough waters they could not watch the cascading blood and still keep their stomachs. Poulsen could, and maybe Steini, the engineer, but they were not like other men.

The male finback lay on the surface, his foreflippers barely moving, his tail motionless. Poulsen called for the stabber, to blow air into the whale so that it would float when they cast it off and went after its mate. He bellowed at his men to hurry.

123

Wanting to get after the female, he watched her, circling the dying whale, then standing off as *Stormur* came broadside and the stabber was smashed in.

The female ran, out from the blood stain that already had spread over two hundred square metres of sea. She spilled her last energy into the chase and then, as Poulsen knew she would, she turned, dashed past the whaler's bows and headed back the way she had come. Soon she was at her mate's side, pushing at him, imploring him to lift his great tail and escape with her. She was still prodding when *Stormur*'s cannon platform loomed overhead, and there was a strange thud and a cloud of smoke in the air, and a fiery pain along her spine.


With the pair of finbacks in tow, *Stormur* made slow progress north by north-east towards her rendezvous. They saw her, even in the high seas, from several miles off: *Ural*, the massive Soviet factory whaler. As *Stormur* approached the cruising giant a great plume of smoke rose from the factory's funnel. She was a floating city, feeding on the last of the great whales in the Atlantic, the tall, steel cliffs of her hull packed with blubber, oil and meat. She had many friends in the northern ocean; pirate whalers from a dozen ports in a dozen countries.

She slid on the sea, drifting like an enormous iceberg, except that she was dark; a rusting, ugly ship, with steam rising from her flensing decks and heat chambers, where the blubber was drained of its oil. A fatty, blood signature followed her and now, as she slowed to a stop, the sea around her fell calm, as if subdued by the presence of the colossus.

Very slowly the lean, fox-like *Stormur* rounded the mountainous hull, moving towards the stern where crew, men and women, were already preparing the dragging apparatus to haul in the whales. Poulsen knew the routine. He hardly needed to watch the bridge where a signaller was guiding him.

This time, however, it was not to be routine. Suddenly a

steam-klaxon was howling. The sea churned at the *Ural*'s stern as her mighty propellers began to turn. On her bridge men were watching to the south through binoculars. With no acknowledgment to the crew of the Faroese whaler, *Ural* was underway.

'There must be a ship out there,' screamed Poulsen. 'Cut the whales loose.' He imagined a fishery vessel speeding up from the south or, worse, a NATO ship spying on the Russian factory. Either way *Stormur* might be seen and that would mean bad trouble, at the very least an end to his licence. He would take her east, into the Norwegian sea. No fishery vessel could catch him, and only the fastest of naval ships. He ran to the wheelhouse. Even as his men were setting loose the whale carcasses, he threw the engines into full ahead. He looked to the south and saw a ship, low on the horizon, almost invisible in the swell and the drizzle that was beginning to fall. In a few minutes the intruding ship was lost to sight and even the *Ural* was diminishing to the west.

Fitzgerald lowered the camera armed with its 1,000 millimetre lens. He shook his head as the rain started to fall more heavily.

'They will not be clear pictures, but the *Stormur* should be recognisable. Not exactly the very best evidence we could have.'

'But in the sea up ahead you will have your evidence,' said Claus quietly. He eased back on *Hannah*'s engine. There was no reason for speed now. Poulsen's ship was below the horizon and would not be returning, and the Russian would not stop to be photographed. 'Now you will see the sort of man Poulsen is.'

They saw, and they found a new hatred for the man who Claus had insisted was the most dangerously insane man in Faroes. At first they said nothing as *Hannah* drifted alongside the massive, air-blown bodies while the sea pushed and tugged at the great fins that once had controlled mighty currents. The female was closest to the trawler and Bowman looked at her

125

grey curves, distorted by the air inside her. She lay on her side. Two thirds of the way down her body towards her tail he saw what appeared to be a long, red gash. But he knew what it was, even before it came closer, before Jens told him. It was like the old nightmare, except that it was real and in the present; mother and child. The baby whale, in its tight amniotic sac, had its eyes closed, as if it were asleep; a perfect, almost ready to be born finback whale, except that it was dead, like its parents.

The strange cortège travelled very slowly south-west towards the Faroe Islands, through the rain and the lumpy seas. The trawler laboured with her great load strung out astern. The four men on board did not speak. A sense of futility and hopelessness enveloped them. There was no point in taking the whales back to Tórshavn, no purpose in showing the authorities what Poulsen had done, or telling them about the encounter with the Russian factory whaler. Yet they would do all those things. Fitzgerald looked at the film reel in his palm. He knew it was the only lasting hope for the whales, if it could get through to an organisation like *World-Watch* who would use the pictures in the media. But that too seemed utterly hopeless. How could a few fuzzy photographs of a Russian factory vessel and a Faroese whaler, even the terrible images of harpooned whales, really show people what was happening in the North Atlantic? They needed to see, smell and feel it for themselves, to hear the screams. They would not believe the photographs, the reality was too far away, in an outland. Even if they believed what they saw, would enough of them care sufficiently to do anything about it?

But he had an idea, one which he had only recently admitted to himself was a possibility. Yet it was, with minor variations, shared at that moment by the three other men on board *Hannah*. It was the only solution to the problem, at least to the local problem of the whaling in the Faroes, the personal situation that had developed for each one of them,

126

and Jákup Poulsen and Eidi, *Stormur*'s crew and the *grind* whalers, the sociable black whales and the finbacks like those in tow; all the terrible, needless waste. There was only one way to stop it.

# 20

'We have intercepted a film', announced the young senior Foreign Office executive as Willoughby entered the room, 'which I thought might interest you. It was sent by your subjects in the Faroe Islands to the *World-Watch* organisation here in London.' He pushed the prints across the table. Willoughby looked at them quickly, then selected a few which had caught his attention.

'Have you identified these ships?'

The official looked offended, as if the fat MI5 man had suggested that the foreign department had overlooked the significance of the ships. 'We believe the small one is a whaler, probably Faroese or Norwegian. You can see that she has whales in tow,' he added, pointing to a smudge near the stern of the ship. 'We are in the process of identifying her positively. There is no doubt about the large one. She is the *Ural*, a Soviet factory vessel. NATO have a thick file on that one.' He noticed that Willoughby had raised a questioning eyebrow. 'Oh, because of her capacity. She could hide an army, or God knows what, inside that hull. She is also an icebreaker, which gives her rapid access to one ocean from another. It is her size more than anything, you understand,' he explained slightly condescendingly. 'She affords the Soviets a considerable presence wherever she is working in the seas of the world. Backed up by a small military fleet, she represents a threat that could not be ignored. Not that there appears to have been any military escort with her when these photographs were taken. Doubtless there will be one of their submarines in the area, or the inevitable Russian trawler.'

'So she's just collecting whales on the high seas from the natives. Illegal, I suppose?' It was an inquiry for more information rather than a question.

'A contravention of International Whaling Commission rules, a breach of international agreement as instigated by the United Nations, not to mention certain foreign trade regulations and Customs control.'

'I see. What action is being taken?' He was looking at the photographs, pausing at the pictures of the dead whales. On the flat prints the whales did not look so very big, or any more prepossessing than any other dead animal. The photographs had the effect of screening the observer from the horrifying reality of what had happened. Willoughby saw just a cold, harsh frame, a misrepresentation of the truth, a fraction of the whole image. He could not hear the bang of the harpoon cannon or the long, drawn-out screams that would penetrate the ocean for a hundred miles. He could not see the churning, scarlet-tainted waters as the whales thrashed. He could not smell them.

'Very little. It is not really our department. NATO has been passed this information, though they probably knew about it already. I would imagine that *Ural* is being shadowed. We have sent on copies of these photographs to the IWC and the roll of film on to *World-Watch*. The Soviet Trade Association has also been informed. We can hardly do more over a few photos of some dead whales.'

'What about Bowman and Fitzgerald?'

'That *was* entirely up to the Danish and Faroese authorities. We had made it clear to Danish Special Branch that if these fellows, and their submarine, simply disappeared and were never heard of again, then it would be as a result of their own foolhardiness. The complication is the Danish trawler, the *Hannah*, and the two Danes . . .' He glanced at the file.

'Hansen and Petersen,' Willoughby reminded him.

'Precisely; but they are Copenhagen's problem.'

'It appears that this whole issue is now somebody else's problem.'

129

The official turned on him. 'Perhaps I should remind you that it was your department that allowed Bowman and Fitzgerald to leave the country in the first place, with,' he added pointedly, 'their wretched submarine.'

'So MI6 is going to let the Danes have them, even though they are obviously working entirely on a conservation issue?'

'Well no, not any more. It's gone a bit too far to leave to some pedantic office in Copenhagen. Your Bowman fellow could carry on for months and cause us considerable embarrassment. He'll hit the media soon, and that just won't do; an Englishman interfering in another nation's concerns at a time when our foreign policies are . . .' he stirred in his seat as if he was uncomfortable at having to explain himself to Willoughby; 'shall we say under stress.'

'What *are* you going to do?'

'Ah, yes, well, Head of Section has passed the message down: "expedient action". We are leaving Hansen and Petersen to the Danish authorities; but Bowman and the American are ours; er, we have CIA approval. Fitzgerald is not exactly popular with . . .'

'Christ, you *can't* do that!' Willoughby was on his feet, leaning forward, his hands bunched into fists on the official's desk.

'Nature of the beast, old chap.' He shrugged. 'They are running out of control, breaking the laws of the land. They have to pay the consequences; no one is immune.'


Willoughby spoke hurriedly to his secretary. 'I want the first flight out tomorrow to Copenhagen and a connection the next day to Vágar in the Faroe Islands. Arrange for a meeting with Danish Special Branch. At Vágar I want a senior police official to meet me.' He was excited; it had been five years since he had worked in the field. Royce, Head of Section, had nearly refused, claiming it to be most irregular; but he, like Willoughby, was intrigued by this affair. Bowman was British and therefore within the domain of MI5. They did not want the Scandinavians, or MI6, to 'bury' him.

*Rozinante* eased across the mouth of the fjord at a depth of forty feet. Bowman watched the depth readings while Fitzgerald concentrated on the sounds he could hear through his headphones. He varied the receiver angle until he picked up the strongest signal. 'Ten degrees off to port; we're quite close.'

Bowman could now hear the rhythmic thumping noise without the aid of headphones. He felt it through the hull of the boat. Fitzgerald, with the receiver apparatus, was able to ascertain the direction in which the sound device lay.

'Dead ahead,' said the American, 'less then twenty metres.' Then they saw it, its weak signal bulb glowing in the dimly lit waters. It was the ninth and last of Fitzgerald's 'thumpers', as they called them, to be exchanged for one with a fresh battery.

They had worked almost continuously for two full days, launching the submarine in dangerous seas, diving, hunting down the sound sources, dropping a fresh thumper and retrieving the old one, before returning to the lee of the trawler where the Danes picked *Rozinante* off the swell with the crane winch. The weather was constantly bad. There seemed as little light on the surface as twenty feet down. Rain fell steadily, now vertically in a great torrent and then driven on the high winds. It meant, at least, that they could work unobserved, for visibility was poor; but they were concerned for the submarine's hull each time she swung out into the battering swell. Her repaired nose section and seals, after the accident off Suduroy, had performed perfectly, although Bowman had not attempted a deeper dive than sixty feet. None of the thumpers lay more than fifty feet below high tide level.

It was the end of June and still there had been no *grind* since May. Whales had been sighted, but always too far off-shore to herd them into the fjords. The islanders were surprised and frustrated that the schools would not approach those areas where they were most usually found, but the whalers did not suspect that the Danes or the two foreigners on *Hannah* were responsible. They blamed the weather, the continuous succession of violent squalls from the south and west, or the lateness of the summer after a prolonged, foggy spring; anything but the little, innocuous trawler. Only Jákup Poulsen was close to the truth, and his own particular type of solution.

The incident with the finbacks and *Ural* had been uncomfortable and he had lost face to the authorities; all because of Claus Hansen who had brought the evidence in to Tórshavn. There was a terrible rage that struggled within Poulsen. It was focused upon the trawler and the men who worked on her. It was too calculating to be total insanity, too violent to belong to any ordinary man. As it grew it consumed him, forcing everything from his mind except the overpowering need for revenge, final and absolute. Furthermore, he was certain that the subjects of his hatred were also responsible for the scarcity of the *grindvhal* close to shore. 'They are clever conservationist rats,' he told Steini, the engineer. 'They keep the whales away from us somehow; away from the fjords. We stop them Steini? We sink their boat, Ja? Maybe the rats leave the sinking ship, eh, and we watch them drown?'


At a depth of thirty feet the *Rozinante* turned out of Sörvágsfjorður, into the face of the current. She bucked in turbulence and then settled as the motors whined at three-quarters power. Bowman closed his eyes for several seconds, taking an emotional grip on himself. He had been diving too much, a dread of the deep water developing more strongly each time they dropped from the trawler, each time the tanks flooded. You needed a recovery time after the peculiarly exhausting effects of a dive. The fears could be forced away for a while, until they became too concentrated and repeated too many times. Then your heart raced during every manoeuvre, every sound was exaggerated; the creaks of the reinforced glass fibre were like tearing sounds, the bang as the panels went concave possessed some dreadful finality, a drip from a seal was the prelude to a sudden rupture.

He fought the fears continuously, but they preyed on him. He recognised his growing instability and realised that he was endangering the vessel while it was submerged. He did not know whether or not his judgements could be trusted. Would he panic during those moments when his decisions needed the most precision, when currents blasted without warning off the sea floor or the spinning waters near the surface grappled with the boat? And yet he had to carry on, for none of the others had the experience to control the boat in such seas. It would be suicide. The responsibility, however, of having his best friend at his side, while Bowman desperately struggled to stave off the doubts and the fears, only added to his traumas.

He concentrated on the monitor screen. *Hannah*'s recognisable signal blipped where he expected it to be. That was reassuring, knowing that the trawler was never far away, that the machinery was working so well, that he had successfully navigated the boat in and out of yet another fjord. Best of all their actions were keeping the whales away out to sea. The thumpers worked, as did the means by which they were maintained; but the dangers, and the strain on a man's mind, were extreme.

Fitzgerald glanced at the Englishman, a twinge of fear in his own stomach. He, unlike Bowman, had managed to master the peculiar sensations he experienced during a dive; but then his own activity, that of finding the thumpers and maintaining the acoustic apparatus, always occupied his mind. The control of the submarine was not his, although his trust in his friend's abilities was total, and he was a fatalist. Now, however, as he saw the sweat on Bowman's brow, and the taut expression, he understood the man's inner battle. Both their lives lay in the care of those trembling hands, and the rationale and courage of the mind behind that stressed façade.

Close to the stormy surface the waters growled over the fragile hull. The boat was rolling and the motors whined haphazardly as the propellers bit first on water, then on foam or air. It was far worse than when they had launched, thought Bowman; the worst conditions in which they had yet worked

133

the submarine. The vibration and roll were sickening as the relentless forces threatened to tear the boat apart. Then she surfaced and a long swell passed over her. Bowman increased the motor speed and turned the boat until she faced the open sea where *Hannah* stood off, upwind. Driving hard at the running seas *Rozinante* slowly made headway. Each time her nose came up a plume of spray cut into the rain-filled air, and she staggered down into the troughs.

Bowman glanced over at Fitzgerald and shook his head.

'It's no good,' he shouted. 'We'll have to dive again and wait until this dies down a bit. They'll never manage to hook us out in this.' The American nodded as Bowman's hands moved to the ballast valves.

It was a relief to fall back down into the quiet and calm of the sea. The boat settled at forty feet, suspended over deep water. She was a hundred metres down-drift of the anchored trawler. The batteries were less than half charged. Bowman switched off all the lighting and acoustic apparatus. Only the monitor glowed a feeble, warm red as the sonar circle swept around the screen.

'Now we wait,' said Bowman as trickles of sweat ran down his temples. The motors murmured as he let them slowly turn, keeping the boat stationary, facing the current.

'How long can we wait?'

'Like this, quite a long time, six hours, maybe longer, so long as I don't need to run the motors any faster. It's one o'clock now. We will have to surface by about seven, come what may.' As if from far away they heard the storm, carving out the surface of the sea. Beyond the viewing windows was an impenetrable darkness. Bowman stared into the void. His imagination told him of terrors that hid out there, nightmares that would soon be reality; a cold, high pressure space where creatures lurked, waiting. Suddenly he spoke. 'I can't hold it together much longer, George. My nerve's going.'

'Nothing's changed, Son; you're tired, that's all,' came the comforting, warm drawl.

'I'm losing trust in myself. There are too many things to think about driving this boat, in too short a space of time.'

'Yeah, well you don't have to do anything for a few hours now.' His words were firm. 'Go to sleep. I can hold her in position and will wake you if anything happens.' Even as the American spoke Bowman's eyes were closing as his mental exhaustion gave in gratefully to sleep under Fitzgerald's influence. The images of the dark, cold deep disappeared while the muscles of his face relaxed and his trembling ceased.

Fitzgerald sighed and sat back into the foam rubber. He too was tired, but his was not a mind-preying exhaustion. He had not had to battle with the violent Faroese tides. He wondered how Bowman had managed for so long; a month of diving, virtually every day, and the work on the surface, maintaining the battery charger and air-compressor, tending the hull and seals, studying the charts, planning . . . Bowman had worked too hard, checking and rechecking every manoeuvre, the sections of glass fibre, minutely examining the submarine's every detail, and then enduring for so long the terrible dangers underwater. It was not only the Germans who were capable of training people to such painstaking levels of precision. Fitzgerald caught himself smiling. It was odd how the British could exist with their general acceptance of mediocrity, and yet could produce a very few men like Bowman.

*Hannah*'s deck tilted alarmingly as another vast swell swept beneath the hull, lifting her and smashing her down, jarring her wooden frame. The storm had built so suddenly. In less than half an hour, while *Rozinante* had been submerged, the wind had built from a relatively comfortable Force four to a nine, kicking up the waves and stampeding them into the confined waters of the west-facing fjord.

'We have to lift the anchor,' shouted Claus. 'She cannot stand much more of this. Our friends have gone down and will wait; perhaps they will follow us. We must run off-shore.' The engine coughed and caught and the trawler piled into the massive seas.

Down below, Fitzgerald watched as the blip on the screen

135

faded and then intensified, drawing very slowly away from the centre of the circle. He reached over Bowman and turned up the power to the motors, then held the steering column to guide the submarine. The sleeping man did not stir while his machine pushed through the Atlantic and the batteries gradually drained their power.


Through the rain Claus saw the little island of Gáshólmur about two kilometres to the south. Between that and the island of Tindhólmur was a narrow sound. He knew the place. In a wind from the south or north it was a spilling race of water; but in other winds it was calm, sheltered by the peak of Tindhólmur and the mound of Gáshólmur. In that storm it might afford sanctuary, and a chance to pick up the submarine.

Fitzgerald turned *Rozinante* to follow the trawler's signal. It was three in the morning now and he glanced at the top left-hand corner of the screen where the battery condition was recorded. They had less than a quarter of their charge remaining. If he followed *Hannah* much farther he would exhaust the batteries. He woke Bowman.

'You can still hear the storm raging up there,' he said as the Englishman stretched and yawned. 'We can't go up yet; but we're using too much battery.'

'Christ, we are, George,' said Bowman as he too glanced at the screen. 'We shall have to stop. What's Claus up to?'

'There's land up ahead. Maybe he's running in to find shelter.' They looked at the chart. 'We are somewhere here,' he pointed to a position north of the islets. Claus must be moving towards that deep channel.' Again they watched the screen. At the very top of the circle was a smudge which they guessed was the north shore of Tindhólmur. 'Almost a kilometre and a half,' said Fitzgerald. 'Can we make it?'

Bowman grated his teeth as he struggled with a decision which normally he would have made with little hesitation. They had just enough power to reach the channel, provided he ran the motors carefully and did not make any mistakes; but it was dangerous. There were no guarantees that Claus would be able to pick them up in the channel, and their batteries would be almost drained. Even their air would be low. If they waited where they were the storm might outlast their capacity to remain submerged. Sometimes high winds raged for days on the Faroes banks. Either way there was risk. 'We'll be all out when we get there. If the tide's too strong in that channel then we'll be pushed wherever it wants us to go. Claus will know we're following him. He will be able to see from up top if the currents are too powerful for us, in which case he won't go in. We have to trust to luck, George.'

'So what's new?'

Bowman slightly increased the motor speed and they moved slowly southwards. Ahead and above, the trawler pitched in the powerful swell. Claus turned the helm to meet each run of high crests, then eased her back off to the south. Gáshólmur was almost lost in the heavy rain and rushing waves.

Neither of the Danes watched out to the west, towards the island of Mykines, where the grey Fisheries' patrol vessel skulked, and the whaler, *Stormur*, split the great seas driving at her pointed bows.

It took an hour to reach the wave-thrashed shores of the islets. Just as Claus had foreseen, the channel lay sheltered. It heaved with a big groundswell, but there were no wind-blown waves. *Hannah* came about as Jens prepared to drop anchor. Then Claus shouted from the wheelhouse.

'Stop, Jens.' He pointed towards the channel's entrance. 'It's *Stormur*!' Both men looked aft to see the whaler pushing past Gáshólmur. Materialising from the rain behind her was the Fisheries' vessel, a converted minesweeper. Both ships were heading straight for the drifting trawler. Claus swore. 'Jákup has led them to us. Now he works with the *Politi*, Jens. He has begun to take his revenge.' He looked around the channel. 'I hope our friends do not come up just yet.'

The air was hissing into the ballast tanks as *Rozinante* began her ascent from forty feet. It was Fitzgerald who feverishly closed the valves and released the air. 'Look, the screen . . . .

two signals to stern. They're coming in fast. What are they?'

'Large; they're not fishing boats; and they're coming our way.' Bowman glanced at the depth reading. They were already below forty feet and falling rapidly. The sea bed was another sixty feet below them. Bowman switched the sonar to passive and the screen immediately lost all signals but one: the vessel farther out at the mouth of the channel. 'That must be military, or a Customs launch. It's equipped with a search sonar. We'll have to sit on the sea floor to hide; if they haven't seen us already.'

They fell; eighty feet, eighty five . . . Bowman reopened the air line to slow their descent. Briefly he switched on the flood lamp to illuminate the approaching floor. They caught a glimpse of bare boulders before the lamp was extinguished. The air rushed and the submarine levelled and hung, feet above the floor. Then she bumped on hard rock and came to rest. Bowman switched everything off except the passive sonar and they sat silently on the floor of the channel, watching the lone blip approaching the screen's centre. Both men knew that the power was almost exhausted and the reserves of air, also, were nearly drained. They waited.

# 21

Dalsgaard, the captain of the Fisheries' vessel, had boarded *Hannah* with three of his men. He spoke in Danish. 'You are Claus Hansen?' Then, indicating towards where Jens was making fast the ropes which were holding the two boats together, 'And he is Jens Petersen?' Claus nodded. 'Where are your other crew members, please?'

'Jens is my crew.'

'We know that you have two other men, an Englishman and an American. Where are they?'

'Those men are sometimes my crew, when I need some help with my fishing. As you can see, they are not with me now.'

'They were seen boarding this boat yesterday afternoon in Tórshavn.'

'Did Jákup tell you that?' Dalsgaard did not answer.

'Where are those men?'

'We put them off at Vestmanna. Would you like a drink, Captain, before you leave my boat?' The Fisheries' officer felt threatened as the tall Dane stood over him.

'This is not a game, Hansen. My men will search this boat, while you explain to me what you are doing out here.'

Claus raised his hands. 'I have nothing to hide.' He watched Dalsgaard's men entering the forward cargo hold. He wondered if they knew what they were looking for down there. Poulsen would not have been able to tell them; no matter what he suspected, he did not know about the submarine. Would, therefore, the Fisheries' men realise the significance of the air compressor or the battery unit? Would they notice the acoustic

139

apparatus spread around the trawler? Dalsgaard would notice, Claus felt sure of that from the look of intelligence in the man's eyes, but the captain was not searching. 'We are sheltering from the storm, Captain. It is very rough out there and we cannot fish in weather like this, you understand.'

'Taking shelter; you are doing nothing else here?' asked Dalsgaard smoothly. At that moment a young man who was the wireless operator on the Fisheries' vessel entered *Hannah*'s wheelhouse. He walked directly over to Dalsgaard, stooped and spoke quietly into the captain's ear. Dalsgaard smiled, his stare fixed on the Dane. 'Perhaps it would make me happier if you accompanied us to Tórshavn, where we can search this boat properly.'

'You are arresting me?' Outwardly Claus was unperturbed; but his mind was racing. Somewhere down in the sea, not far away, were his friends. If he was arrested now he would be leaving them to the mercy of the storm. He could not risk that. His tone was less arrogant than before, conciliatory. 'You can see that my boat cannot leave this channel while the wind is so strong. She would be broken up by those seas. I will come with you, if you wish, while Jens remains on *Hannah*. But I do not understand why you want me. There is nothing I can tell you in Tórshavn that I cannot tell you here.' Dalsgaard laughed loudly.

'Perhaps I should tow your trawler, eh?' He frowned in mock severity. 'Or should I leave my men on board to look after her while you and Petersen accompany me to harbour?'

'But what is it you want of . . .' The men had come up from below. One of them shook his head at the captain. Dalsgaard stood up from the helm chair.

'Very well,' he said abruptly; 'I will think about this. You will wait here, please.' With that he left them, his men following him out on to the deck and across to the Fisheries' boat.

'He knows, Jens. Somehow he knows, I am sure of it.' Claus looked across the gloomy, rain-lashed waters to where *Stormur* was standing off. 'And what has that bastard to do with all this?

maybe he knows also; but this is not his way, to work with the Politi.'

Willoughby, feeling more than a little seasick, made to stand as Dalsgaard and the wireless operator entered the bridge. The captain motioned him to be reseated. 'Hansen and Petersen are on board. My man here tells me that he observed a weak echo from an unidentified, submerged object as we pulled into this channel. I believe that object was the submarine you suspect them of possessing, probably with Bowman and the American on board.'

'And what did your men find on the trawler?'

'Machinery which could maintain and service a small submarine, some electronic and acoustic apparatus . . .'

'Where is that submarine now?' asked the fat SIS man. He gripped the sides of his chair as another swell heaved the ship over to starboard.

'Probably right below us, sitting on the bed about a hundred feet below our keel.' He looked at the wireless operator for confirmation of his supposition. The man nodded his agreement. 'So we have them. What do you want me to do?'

Willoughby thought for a few moments. After a thorough briefing with the Faroese Politi he had the unquestioning support of Dalsgaard. That was something, but there were complications: Poulsen, who had been so keen to pass on information about the recent activities of the men on board *Hannah* and then had agreed too readily to assist the authorities in finding the Danish trawler. Now that they had found her what was there to be gained by arresting her crew, even in waiting for the submarine to surface and impounding that? So far the Danes, Bowman and Fitzgerald had apparently done no more than witness a malpractice between a Faroese whaler and a Soviet factory vessel; and that whaler was Poulsen's *Stormur*, he was sure of it, even if Intelligence had been unable to confirm that fact. There was more to the whole issue than this. If he moved now he would have nothing but a handful of renegades who had directed their energies and concerns on slightly the wrong side of the law. It was not enough; not worth SIS involvement.

And then there was the MI6 operative to consider. The Foreign Office man had told him of the 'expedient action'. Somewhere on the islands was a killer, waiting for the moment when he could finish the entire affair – with two high-velocity bullets.

'Leave them, Captain; shadow them, find out what they are up to. I want to know everything they do. And that whaler; there is more to him than meets the eye.'


Condensation poured from the glass fibre and the viewing ports. Both men were sweating in the stifling, stale atmosphere. It was fear as much as the fact that Bowman, in order to preserve their precious positive ballast, had closed the cabin release valve. Their ears hurt as the cabin pressure increased and their hearts rapidly pumped to compensate for the increased levels of carbon dioxide in their blood. They had been on the sea floor for two hours, watching the monitor screen informing them of the dwindling battery power, the last reserves of air; their dying boat, far down in the dark, cold sea.

Now, at last, the ships on the surface had gone, except for the trawler. Not that it mattered any more, for if they did not attempt to surface at that moment they would never do so. Bowman, eyes closed with the pain in his head, gripped the first air valve to the ballast tanks. He turned and there was a weak, almost inaudible hiss, then nothing. *Rozinante* did not stir. He felt for the other valve and turned that too. There was a stronger gush of air and the boat staggered and lifted very slowly from her rocky bed. Bowman opened his eyes, his fears suddenly doubled. There was not enough air! He had miscalculated; the submarine would not reach the surface at her present rate of ascent. She would achieve a neutral bouyancy at fifty or sixty feet, stranded in the mid-deep. Their only chance lay in there being sufficient charge remaining in the batteries for him to drive the motors as fast as they would go, keeping the submarine's nose into the current. Then, with the diving plane fully elevated, they might gain enough lift.

Bowman caught himself hoping that Claus and Jens were alert. If *Rozinante* reached the surface, she would only stay there as long as the motors drove her. As soon as they stopped she would sink. He reckoned they would need to hook up the crane winch on the very first pass. The screen recorded an almost zero battery charge. It was unlikely that the submarine would have enough power to reach the surface, let alone closely approach the trawler. Certainly there could not be a second attempt.

He was aware of the sound of his breathing, harsh and fast. His throat was sore and his head felt as if there was something inside, pushing on the cranium. *Rozinante* had floated up to the hazy blue layers of the sea, but she hung there, almost stationary at a depth of more than forty feet. Bowman stared at the screen, as if hypnotised by it. There was the blip, very close to the circle's centre. That was the trawler; but there was a fog across his eyes and nothing made sense now as the carbon dioxide poisoning increased.

Almost instinctively he turned the motors' power to maximum and held the diving plane hard down. He heard the whine, intense at first, then gradually diminishing. The blue light had become grey and white. He could hear the sound of rain as the submarine was caught by a swell. She broke through the surface and still the propellers turned. Fitzgerald began to open the seal clamps.

'No, George,' yelled Bowman, 'not yet, we'll lose buoyancy. We have to wait.'

They both saw the trawler at the same time, just twenty metres off to port. The motors' whine was slight now and Bowman felt the boat losing steerage way. He flung the rudder hard over, but she barely responded. A swell covered her and then, again, she struggled through into the air.

Claus had been alert and watchful. At full astern he backed the trawler towards the wallowing submarine. Jens was already swivelling out the crane rig with its specially adapted hook.

143

Claus knew that his crew man would not miss, or if he did he would dive in and hook her up.

The rain stamped heavily on the wheelhouse roof. There was no wind and the swell was flatter than before. The men talked, the two submariners both rubbing their temples in an effort to remove the last remnants of headache after the carbon dioxide poisoning.

'So they know,' repeated Claus. 'We will have to act immediately, with whatever time there is left.' As an afterthought he added: 'It might not be enough.'

'Son,' moaned Fitzgerald, 'there is never enough time; but, you see, you have to use what time there is to the best effect. Besides, half an hour ago, when my English pal here was trying to drive that damn boat at the surface, I was sure as hell that time had run out.'

**22** Rounding the cliff-banked headland of Rív-tangi, north Esturoy, the trawler made steady progress on the calm sea. She disturbed a raft of feeding puffins that rose noisily into the washed-out sky. The four men were tired since the incident with the finback whales and were feeling the strain of not knowing what might happen next. Claus was looking aft every few minutes.

'I know that Fisheries' boat is still there,' he said; 'Dalsgaard is too clever to let us get away so easily. He knows too much, and suspects the rest.' Then he turned to Bowman. 'We will drop you off as fast as we can near the caves. I should be able to lose the Fisheries' boat among the outer fjords. There are few people in the area, but fishermen going down to Kalksvík use the channel. It should be quietest in the early hours of the morning.' He paused as he glanced at the charts and took a bearing from landmarks on Kalsoy and Esturoy. 'Are you sure you do not want me to return for you and for us to go about this thing another way? There is much distance between Kunoy and Tórshavn for you to travel in your submarine.'

'No, you must be in Tórshavn from the day after tomorrow,' replied Bowman. 'If you are there then so will Jákup be. It is essential for us that *Stormur* is in her usual berth. We cannot afford any accidents and I doubt if there will be another chance. We must keep to our plan; it is our only hope of success.' He spoke quickly, almost feverishly, as he impressed upon his friends the necessity of keeping to the plans they had made. Now, as well as all the odds, time was also against them. He knew that British Intelligence, or whoever it was that had taken such keen interest in their activities in Scotland, must have informed the Faroese authorities of their suspicions. Somehow they had linked the trawler with him and Fitzgerald.

They were fortunate the Fisheries' vessel had backed off and given them this last chance, even if it were so slight. It would cost them, in terms of risk and courage, more than anything that had already happened; but it was their biggest chance of all. They had stopped the pilot whale hunting. Now they would put an end to Poulsen's piratical hunting of the finbacks for the Russians, and there was only one way to do it.

Bowman smiled. 'In three days' time, my friends, it will all be over. For better or worse, our work here will be finished.' He felt a tremendous relief as he spoke the words. It gave a finite target for which to aim. He had to control his fears for just another three days; not so very long compared with all the hours he and Fitzgerald had spent submerged since their arrival in Faroes. 'We can manage that, can't we, George?'

'Son, can it be worse than our last little dive?'

It could, thought Bowman. Every drop was, for him, more terrifying than the one before; the living nightmare of the cold, dark deep more intense, the way his senses were keener, the sounds louder, the shadows more often filled with figments, his fears more tangible and immediate. And this last, long dive was to be the most dangerous of them all, taxing him more than any other; the biggest dive of his life. He turned to Claus. 'Just make sure that everyone is off the *Stormur* by ten in the morning. You will signal us when the whaler is empty by dropping a thumper into the water.' It sounded so ridiculously simple and yet they all knew it was unlikely to be like that. There were too many variables, too many parts of their plan which had flaws, for there was no time to check every detail to make it even approach being fail-safe.

Kallur headland, like a great, stumbling animal lurching into the sea, lay a kilometre to the south. Claus turned the helm to direct *Hannah* towards the massive northern point of Kunoy. The brilliant sunshine intensified the colours which had been dulled to shades of grey during the storm. Now the Faroes were

146

incandescent and vital, a mountain range rearing from the deep Atlantic, necklaced by the foam of breaking waves, warmed by the mid-summer sun. The archipelago of Viking myth and saga appeared as a welcoming refuge among the wastes of ocean, as it must have been for the Irish monks who were the first settlers, then soon afterwards for those aggressive explorers in their Long Ships. Then a visitor's eyes saw the dark crevices in the towering cliffs, the high, grassy, treeless slopes reaching up to the wind-torn mountains' summits, the peat bogs and naked rock, an uncultivable land of mists and storms where a fine summer's day when a warm wind blew was treasured.

'Hunting weather,' announced Claus; 'the islanders will be looking to the sea for some sport as long as this fine weather holds. We, and the storms, have starved them of their fun for a long while. Now they will be bored. This is a good time, my friends, to give them something else to think about. We will give them all the sport they need, eh?'

None of them, thought Bowman, appeared to have given any consideration to the future beyond the next few days. This last effort was the whole future, all of it that mattered. He had not even thought about Vicky during the recent hectic days of their venture, and yet he had always wondered about the times they would eventually share together. He had imagined that the future held something better than those years they had already shared. But it was impossible now: ridiculous.

Claus would surely be thinking of Eidi, dreaming that they would have some time when they did not need to meet in secrecy, when they could enjoy a freedom away from the malice of her brother. Yet Claus was risking as much as the rest of them, perhaps more, for he was risking Eidi's love for him.

Fitzgerald had already lived on the edge, exploring life beyond the experience of most men. Even so one could not imagine that the big, jovial American had no remaining ambitions other than putting an end to commercial whaling. And Jens, the quiet, straggly-haired enigma, who rarely spoke; the competent, fair-skinned man with his considerable appetite for women – how did he visualise his own future?

147

The trawler entered Haraldsund and crept away from the open sea.

'It is only another few kilometres to the caves,' said Claus. 'Get everything ready on deck. We must be very quick. Then Jens and I can run *Hannah* down into the fjords and lose that Fisheries' vessel. They have been watching us on radar; I am sure of it. Here the coast will hide us, for ten minutes at least.'

It took them all that time, and a little more, to transfer the sections of *Rozinante* to the cave where Claus and Jens had hidden the equipment during the late winter. Rather than carry the heavy batteries into the cave they hid them close to the beach. They watched the entrance to the fjord as they worked, but nothing approached, and *Hannah*, moored so close to land, would not be visible on a radar screen. As Claus prepared to push off the skiff he hesitated and turned to Bowman and Fitzgerald.

'The next time we see one another will be when our work is over.' His wide smile was infectious. 'It has been a good adventure, Ja?'

'Mad bastard Dane,' said Fitzgerald, 'I think your smuggling days in these waters are over.'

'There are other lands where we can smuggle; but anyway, we are tired of the running, Jens and I. This has been the last run.'

'So what about that lady of yours?'

'I will worry about Eidi, my friends.'

Fitzgerald put out his hand to shake Claus's, but the Dane opened his arms and hugged the big American, then turned to Bowman and did the same. 'My *good* friends; you did not let me down. After you do this last thing your own lives will change as much as ours. You are outlaws.'

Claus watched the two figures standing on the beach as the skiff pulled out towards the trawler. 'They are the bravest men I ever knew, Jens. The Englishman has become what the Greenlanders call "sea-shy", and yet he continues to dive.' He felt a heavy sadness descend upon him as the two men on the beach waved. *Hannah* seemed curiously empty without them, without all the electronic gadgetry and the odd camaraderie they had shared. The trawler's engine caught and she began to back away from the shore. 'It was such an ambitious idea, Jens. No one would have thought we would have brought it this far. It was a *grand* idea.'

He forced himself to look away down the fjord, towards the narrows north of Klaksvík. Now he would weave the trawler among the outer isles until he had lost any Fisheries' boat that might be watching. Then he would take her to Tórshavn, and Eidi, and prepare for the big gamble.

**23** It was gloomy and cold in the cave. Right up at the back, where the crevice became too thin for a man to pass through, they found the pile of old driftwood and rotten weed beneath which were the waterproofed crates Claus and Jens had left there, three months earlier. Gingerly, Fitzgerald passed them out to Bowman.

'No need to take such care, George. The stuff is inert. It needs to be detonated.'

'How much we got?'

'Ten kilos; enough, believe me.'

They unwrapped all the contents of the crates and spread them out over the cave's floor. In all there were twenty-two blocks of explosive, nitroglycerine soaked into clay, as well as detonator chemicals consisting of powdered aluminium, crystalline iodine, and an oxidising agent, potassium dichromate, together with various materials for assembly of the device they were going to use. Fitzgerald shook his head.

'You had this all worked out, didn't you? You *knew* we were going to use this stuff.'

'I suspected it would come to this, yes. So did you. We talked about it a great deal before we decided to go ahead. You and I both hoped we would not need to do this; but, as we can all see, it is now the only way. If we sink that whaler it will be the biggest news ever to come out of Faroes.' He lowered his voice as the sound echoed hollowly around the rocky chamber. 'The media will exaggerate it all and will focus attention on the whaling that goes on out here. No one, outside these islands, knows about the pirate whaling or the selling of finbacks to the Russians on the high seas. Well, our photos, provided they get through to *World-Watch*, will show them what's going on; but it needs something spectacular to grab people's attention.'

'If we hurt anyone,' said the American, pensively, 'it will do more harm than good.'

'Which is why, George, we will place the charge deep below *Stormur*'s water-line. We will detonate it when no one is aboard. Her bows are always pointing out to sea – one of Jákup's habits – so we will place it there, away from the quayside. Claus will drop the thumper when everyone is away from the boat. If we don't hear the signal we take the charge out to sea and dump it on the floor.'

'If we don't hear that thumper we'll fail. As you say, the photos will not be enough. They will only mean something to those people who already know what is happening. A whaler blown from the water is the sort of news to grab everyone's attention.' Fitzgerald sighed heavily. 'It's a sick world when you have to do something like this to make everyone take notice.'


'We have lost the trawler, Mr Willoughby,' announced Dalsgaard as he walked into the bridge ante-room. 'She is somewhere among these fjords, but it is impossible to follow a ship in this area unless we can maintain visual contact. Our radar is useless so close in-shore. We have, however, found something which might interest you.'

'Well, what is it?' asked Willoughby irritably.

'An underwater sound source on the sea bed about fifty feet down. The sonar operator heard it. I sent a diver down to investigate.'

'Where did you find it?'

'Here, at the entrance to the little fjord that leads up to Klaksvík.'

'And this sound source is nothing to do with the Fisheries, or any military activity?'

'Not that I know of, Sir. My diver fixed a line to the device and we have hauled it up on to the deck. Would you like to see it?'

On deck, the small device appeared insignificant, except that every ten seconds it emitted a harsh, cracking sound.

'Do you have any idea what it is?' asked the Englishman.

'You are the Intelligence man,' replied Dalsgaard, with a shrug.

'I asked you a question, Captain.'

Dalsgaard eyed the man with whom he had been ordered to co-operate. He wondered why Danish Special Branch had not sent an overseer. Why a British SIS man? It was politics, he supposed; keeping the NATO powers happy, in the same way that the islanders on Stremoy had to tolerate the presence of the listening station on the high mountain above Kaldbaks-fjórður.

'I suspect it was placed here by your Bowman, or his friends. I am not sure what purpose it serves; possibly to guide them when they are underwater.'

Willoughby smoothed his hands over the stubble on his heavy jowls. Dalsgaard was half-right, he thought, but the device was not to guide the submarine. Suddenly, as he turned sharply away to affect his lack of interest, he said, 'It is a whale scarer. Drop it back overboard, please.' He walked to his cabin. As he closed the door behind him he permitted himself a smile. They were clever, the men he had come to Faroes to investigate. They had not only built a submarine, but also other apparatus to help them accomplish a difficult task. He wondered whether or not the sound device – or devices (surely they would have deployed more than one) were effective. He supposed they must have been, for he had heard during his investigations of the mysterious absence of the *grindvhal*, even though it was the height of the season. What else had Bowman and Fitzgerald constructed? Just what could their submarine achieve? So far they had evaded all the authorities; but he was getting very close now. He felt he was beginning to under-stand the way these men thought. He had seen the photographs of the Soviet whaler and the dead whales, and had studied the histories of both Bowman and Fitzgerald. Their past was no secret to him and their present was becoming clearer. The sound device had not been a surprise to him. It had merely supplied another part of the jigsaw. It was a fascinating case, but he was breaking it.

Then he frowned. The MI6 killer would also be close. Maybe, even now, he was ahead of Willoughby, ahead of them all. Where was this killer? Who was he? Was it too late to stop him, to get Bowman and the American out of the Faroes? There could not be much time.

He wondered how it would end. If he had been Bowman how would he end it? Instinctively he knew that Bowman was the organiser, and also that the affair was approaching its conclusion; but what would happen next?

He felt the ship lurch as it sped out into open sea. Dalsgaard was, no doubt, heading off-shore so that he could give his radar a chance to find the Danish trawler. Willoughby knew the captain was wasting his time. Only Bowman or the killer could take the next step.

All through that day the last device was being constructed, close to the cave entrance on Kunoy. The two men worked quietly as they concentrated on their particular task, Bowman in assembling the explosive and detonator in a watertight container, while Fitzgerald worked on the timer and wiring for triggering the device.

Packed into a cavity within the central block of explosive was a ground powder mixture of heat-sensitive chemicals and an oxidising agent. Embedded in this was a glass vial containing a material which, when mixed with the powder surrounding it, would cause the sudden generation of a large amount of heat. Attached to this vial was Fitzgerald's simple electronic system which would cause the glass to shatter and thereby mix the chemicals. The resultant heat generated would be more than enough to detonate the explosive.

153

That evening Bowman packed the entire device into Plasticine and then into polythene bags to keep it dry when it was immersed in the sea, where it would be for twelve hours. He then strapped two heavy magnets to the bundle which would hold it to *Stormur*'s steel hull. A single wire came out of the bundle which, when pulled free, would activate Fitzgerald's five-minute timer.

The two men looked at their crude, delayed-action limpet mine.

'Now we have to treat it very carefully,' said Bowman. 'If a heavy shock were to break that vial it wouldn't be very long before enough heat was generated to detonate the explosive.'

'A charming little device,' intoned Fitzgerald. 'Let's hope for a smooth passage to Tórshavn.'

**24** Motionless in the calm weather, *Hannah* lay moored among all the colourfully painted, high-prowed fishing boats in Tórshavn west-side. In the warm light thrown from the oil lamp in his cabin Claus lay thinking, Eidi sleeping at his side, her head on his shoulder. It was a little after midnight and the harbour was quieter than usual, bathed in a misty twilight. The big whaler still had not returned and it was this that concerned Claus. If all was well, his friends would soon be leaving Kunoy for their long journey down to Tórshavn; twelve hours it should take them, but the effort would be wasted if *Stormur* was not moored up by the time they arrived.

While the whaler was away, however, he and Eidi could be together. She stirred and opened her eyes.

'Why is Jákup helping the Politi, Eidi?' he asked.

'Because they were looking for you. He wants to give you trouble. He is probably furious now because they did not arrest you.'

'It was close; they know too much. I think they are waiting until they have more evidence against us. God knows what Jákup has told them.'

'They will not take too much notice of what he says after that whaling business. They know you did not shoot those finbacks and that he has the only ship in these islands capable of doing such a thing. He told me that you were trying to frame him. He has told the Politi the same thing, and that there was no Russian factory ship, but they will not believe him.'

'Neither will they do anything to stop him doing it again.' He

155

looked at her face. 'We are going to stop him, my friends and I. When is he returning to harbour?'

'I expect him back early this morning.' She closed her eyes again. 'How are you and your friends going to stop him?' He did not answer, but stroked his fingers through her hair, hoping that she would not ask him again, for he could not lie to her, even over this, and yet he did not want to tell her what they had planned. 'Promise me you will not hurt him. Whatever he has done, you must not hurt him. It would be like hurting a wicked little boy. Nothing is achieved by such a thing.'

Claus stared at her beautiful Icelandic features, the lovely high cheek bones and wide mouth, the smooth, pale skin. He was glad that she had closed her eyes so that she would not see the guilt on his own face. Guilt, because he knew he was lying to her. 'I promise, Eidi. We will not hurt him.'


There was a noise on deck, a footstep. Claus was on his feet in a moment, rushing out of the cabin towards the companionway. He knew it was not Jens returning early. As he reached the wheelhouse a fat man was opening the door.

'Ah,' said the intruder, surprised by the tall, naked Dane, 'I'm so sorry to disturb you, but I think we ought to have a chat. My name's Willoughby. Er, you speak English, don't you?'

'What are you doing on my boat?' growled Claus.

'As I have said, I want to talk to you. It is about Richard Bowman and George Fitzgerald.' He lifted his hands defensively as Claus took a step towards him. 'It's all right, I already know most of it. You smuggled their submarine into these waters. I know about the whale-scarers you have dropped around the islands, the photographs of the *Ural* . . .'

'You are *Politi*?'

'Well now, that's a difficult question. I am not the sort of policeman you might have come across. I work for the British government. Actually I couldn't care less about your smuggling, except that the disappearance of Bowman's submarine from Scotland did cause me some embarrassment. National

156

security is more my line of work.' He smiled as he saw the Dane relaxing. 'No chance of a word with Mr Bowman I suppose?'

'My friends are not here.'

'No, I rather thought not.'

Claus glanced out of the helm windows at the harbour. He noticed the Fisheries' vessel which must have moored up within the last two hours. 'You are with that ship?'

'Yes, I was on board when Dalsgaard visited you off Sörvágsfjörd. That ship is more or less at my disposal while I am here.' He chuckled. 'Rather flattering really. It was I who made sure that you were not arrested.'

'You want me to say thank you?'

'Well you might. I think if you had been arrested then your friends in their submarine might have been in a little trouble. We knew they were down below. There is no need to deny it.' At that moment Eidi climbed up from the companionway hatch. She was dressed in a jumper and skirt. She handed Claus his clothes.

Willoughby stared at her. 'What an enchantingly beautiful woman. Do you speak English, my dear? I'm afraid my Faroese is non-existent.'

'A little,' she replied calmly. 'I understand what you are saying to Claus about his friends.'

'Do you know them?'

'I know they are good men, like Claus.'

'Yes, I'm sure they are. I also believe they are very clever and have strong beliefs, even if they are a little misguided.' He pulled his stare away from Eidi and looked at the Dane. 'We are all misguided, Mr Hansen.'

'Why do you want to talk to Bowman, or to me?' asked Claus.

'Please believe that you have nothing to fear from me. You personally might have nothing to fear from anyone except that the Danish police might not take too kindly to your smuggling; but that is pretty minor, so long as drugs are not involved, and I happen to know they are not. There are things in your favour, especially those photographs of the *Ural*. No Western government is going to take too drastic an action over a straightforward conservation matter . . .'

157

'You make what we do sound small.'

'I don't mean to. Actually I'm impressed by what you have achieved, but I suspect you are on the verge of making a big mistake. As soon as conservationists become involved in what we call terrorism, they become targets for the most unsavoury counter-measures. You understand me?'

Claus understood. 'Why do you think we are going to be treated as terrorists?'

'Don't be ridiculous man; I *know*. Bowman and Fitzgerald are targets. You might be safe, but they have been noticed by my government's counter-terrorist group. Your friends are not terrorists, but as such they will be labelled, so that they can be disposed of conveniently, with impunity. Do you understand *that* Mr Hansen? It is my warning to you, and to my countryman, Bowman; to the American also. Believe me, I know how these matters are dealt with by the authorities.' In the fat man's face, Claus could see a wisdom, an empathy. 'Will you pass on my message to your friends, before it is too late. Dropping whale-scarers around these waters is brilliant. In England and America you will be heroes for it.' There was a peculiar intensity in his eyes. 'Go much further and you will become martyrs.'

Willoughby turned back towards Eidi. He affected a half-bow. 'I am so sorry if I have distressed you, Madam; but there was no other way of informing you all of the situation. Goodnight to you both.' With that he left them, quietly closing the door behind him.


Back in his cabin on the Fisheries' vessel, Willoughby wondered at what he had just done. He had always prided himself on his rational behaviour. He believed he was a good Intelligence man, and yet he had now behaved out of keeping with the normal standards and scope of his work; but then this was no ordinary case. He had become too involved. Certainly he had developed a respect, even a liking, for these men he was investigating. They were not political extremists or activists, or guided by some lunatic religious cause. They were as clever as their courage was obvious. Yes, he liked them. There would be no explaining it to Head of Section, back in London. The Foreign Office would probably have him severely disciplined. He shook his head as he glanced out of the cabin porthole. This place might as well be a million miles from England. The same laws, and structure or order, could not possibly apply. He saw the distant mountains in silhouette against the twilit sky, and the calm, icy waters of the harbour. He thought of the tall Dane and the extraordinarily beautiful woman, then the photographs, the submarine. He was out of place here. He did not belong, and he should not have been imposing the ways of another nation far away.

And out there, somewhere on the islands, probably in Tórshavn, was another employee of Her Majesty's government. That thought frightened Willoughby.

None the less he felt good. He had done the right thing in warning Claus Hansen.

**25** It was three in the morning and the fjord lay silky calm. A fine mist hung along the lower slopes of Kunoy where the two men worked, carrying their machinery to the water's edge. The sound of the submarine's clip bolts closing was unnaturally loud in the still air. One by one the heavy batteries were loaded and the wiring connected. The boat took longer than usual to assemble, for there were extra batteries and air tanks to stow for the long journey, as well as the explosive device to fit on the nose. The cave was empty at last as Bowman stood in its entrance and looked down to where Fitzgerald held *Rozinante* off the beach.

He hesitated as he tried to stem the old fears. This dive was to be so long, and he was beginning it as a tired man. His stare took in the flat surface of the deep fjord, the apparent calm, the deadly calm. Then he remembered the screams of whales and the way they kicked when the spears were driven into their backs, and how the babies stayed close to their mothers . . . This dive would be for them, and all the cruelty and bloody mess that men had made in the world. Quickly he walked to the beach.

There was little room in the cabin as they jostled themselves into position. Through the mist Bowman could barely see the skyline of the cliffs above and behind them. The area was deserted. He allowed the boat to drift with the hatch open while he checked the monitor and machinery. He engaged the motors at one quarter speed and turned the boat towards the Narrows, far away down the fjord, obscured by mist. There was no sound above the constant whirring of the motors and a slight splash as the propellers bit at the water. The sun shone through intermittent breaks in the low cloud. The landscape, sea and sky, was lit with pastel shades of blue, pink and orange, a sleepy vista of half-shades, eerie, as a mountain peak was seen jutting through a window in the haze.

'We will travel on the surface for as long as we can,' said Bowman. 'When this mist clears, or when we see shipping or a village, we'll have to dive.' Up ahead a salmon cage materialised, floating on the surface. Bowman steered round it as they watched the silver fish lunging across the otherwise calm water. It was extraordinary, he thought, how a nation that had organised its fishing industry better than any other in the world, a leading example in salmon culture, could support the incongruity of the archaic pilot whale hunting. But then, as Claus had explained, Faroes was a nation of inconsistencies, of surprises, of extremes of beauty and ugliness.

At three knots the boat passed down the fjord. By five that morning she was a little north of the Narrows. The mist was only just beginning to clear and the light remained diffuse, the air cool. 'Now we shall have to dive,' said Bowman. 'Away to starboard is the village of Haraldssund. Someone might be watching out to sea.' They pulled down the hatch and clipped it shut. Still running the motors at slow speed, Bowman gradually opened the valves to the ballast tanks. There was a spume of water and foam from the boat's stern as she dug deeper into the surface, like a whale going over after a blow. Then there was just a bow-wave, showing where she pushed through the sea. Soon all marks on the surface were gone and all trace of the submarine had disappeared. At twenty feet she levelled and nudged on through the Narrows.

They were now in some of the most sheltered waters in Faroes, a curving gap of fjord over which towered high mountains on the islands of Kalsoy, Kunoy and Borðoy. Even at a depth of twenty feet the light was dull as the sea lay in the shadow of those looming peaks. Gradually, as the boat turned west, north of Klaksvík, towards Kalsoyarfjörður, the channel opened, the skyline retreated and the light intensified. Still farther, they turned back

161

to the south, into the wide sound dividing Borðoy from Esturoy, and, again, the sea sparkled with a silvery, turbulent glare.

Bowman let *Rozinante* fall another few feet, away from the swirling waters near the surface. Thus far he had been able to run the motors economically, aided by the calm weather and relatively weak currents; but there remained another thirty kilometres to travel and soon they would be in exposed seas. By the time they reached Tórshavn, the batteries would inevitably be low on charge, although it was paramount that he had enough power remaining to manoeuvre the boat towards her target, and then enough to retreat. He turned down the motors so that the boat pushed forwards at only two knots. Fast enough, he thought; fast enough to deliver them.

'I must leave now,' said Eidi. 'He will be returning soon.' It was nearly seven and the harbour was coming to life, fishing boats milling in and out of their moorings on the floating jetties. 'It is late. Someone is bound to see me and will report to Jákup.'

'This time,' said Claus as he hugged her, 'Jákup will have other things on his mind. He will not bully you.'

Eidi's expression was pensive, a little frightened. 'You promised me you would not hurt him.'

'I promised. Now go, Eidi, and see what the day brings.'

As she left, Jens came shambling along the quayside towards the trawler. His tangle of hair was its usual mess, his pullover dragged clumsily over his lean chest. Claus smiled openly. Within an hour the apparent wreck of a man that was Jens Petersen would be ready for whatever adventure or adversity might occur that day. Despite appearances, there was no better man with whom to share dangerous times at sea or in harbour.

Claus watched Eidi walking up the hill away from the quayside, the grey and blue wool of her clothes beautifully set against the curves of her body. Then, as Jens reached the trawler, grinning up at Claus, the woman was gone.

Away across the harbour the Fisheries' vessel was moored,

motionless among the increasing bustle of activity around her. A plume of diesel smoke rose from her stack, demonstrating her readiness, her waiting engines. Claus did not doubt that there was at least one pair of binoculars trained on him at that very moment. He went below with Jens, to prepare for when the whaler arrived.

Cutting sleekly across the becalmed waters *Stormur* approached her mooring. Her bows turned majestically, almost arrogantly, across the face of the harbour. Expertly, Jákup Poulsen eased his ship around so that her stern could back into the mooring. That way her cannon platform stood out towards the sea, like some strange challenge. Claus, watching the whaler being roped up to the quayside, smiled to himself with satisfaction.

'This is right, Jákup; as always you tie your boat so she faces the sea,' he whispered. 'We have hated one another so long that we know each other so well.'

On the whaler, Jákup, also, was thinking of his old enemy. He too looked across the water, towards the trawler and the two figures standing on her deck. He, however, was not smiling. There was, instead, a fierceness in his expression that warned his four crew members of his impending rage. All of them, except Steini, kept away from him and busied themselves with closing up the whaler for her mooring. 'The bastard Danes, Steini,' he spat. 'Where are their conservationist friends, eh? And where is my sister? He has been with my Eidi, last night, I know it, while we were away . . .' The Fisheries' vessel caught his attention. 'We are wasting our time with the *Politi*. They are useless, weak; we do not need their help. I fix those bastards myself: today.'

The three ships lay at the apices of a triangle two hundred metres across. On each vessel were men with shared thoughts and opposed opinion, waiting and brooding. That, really, was like the structure of the Faroes nation against other nations to the south and east, like the whole whaling issue, divided opinion and intense beliefs, with no one giving way to other ideas.

163

# 26

In open sea, east of Esturoy, the boat was riding the currents. Bowman had taken her some distance off-shore to use the natural drift. Soon he would turn her west, in towards Streymoy. Small signals of fishing boats passed across the screen, and the occasional harder blip of a ferry. Fitzgerald dozed as his friend coped with the workings of the submarine. Diving in the half light, the routine hiss of the vent valves, whirring engines, click of the sonar transmitter, was hypnotic. Invariably, one's mind drifted with the peaceful running of the boat; almost silent, just those little sounds that told of normal functioning.

Bowman rubbed the stubble on his chin. He adjusted his position in the foam-rubber seat, trying to rid his body of the little aches that had developed after six hours of diving. For the time being he had overcome his fears. The continuity, the unchanging attitude of the boat, led to a feeling of confidence. Also, they were running shallow, way up in the light layers of the sea, although the apparent safety of this was an illusion created by the light. Deeper, at fifty or sixty feet, away from the hazards on the surface, was a more secure place for a submarine, despite darkness.

He looked at his watch. There were still two more hours before Fitzgerald would take over for a while, so that Bowman could sleep until the final run in to Tórshavn. Examining the monitor he saw that the batteries were coping well with the steady load placed on them from the motors. A strong signal slowly crossed the screen from right to left. That would be a big liner, thought Bowman, setting out across the Norwegian sea.

Just for a moment, when the ship was at its closest position to *Rozinante*, a distance of nearly a kilometre, Bowman could hear the deep rumbling of her massive propellers. He tried not to think of the sweeping blades churning at the sea, like those on the ferry boat which had nearly run into them off Suduroy, the terrible roar and the steel poised only feet above his head.

Studying the chart he judged their position to be far enough south to begin a long, slow swing to the west. The sonar circle was blank. It was tempting to surface, just for some cold air in the lungs and to be able to see a long way. No matter how well one mastered the problem of claustrophobia, a small vessel submerged in the sea was a tight, breathless environment. The risk, however, if he surfaced, was too great; a passing plane, or small fishing boat that had not registered on the sonar, might be up there. It only required one sighting and their great weapon of surprise was lost.

He wondered just how many people knew of the submarine's existence. Claus had been convinced that the Fisheries' vessel captain had known. Had the British informed Danish or Faroese authorities? Had they found a link with the *Hannah*? If they knew, would they then have informed the military? Poulsen had been there, in Sörvágsfjörður. Did he know? Would anyone guess that the boat was to be used as an offensive weapon?

There was no way they could have known about the explosive, because Bowman had made it himself; by pouring glycerine into a glass tank containing concentrated nitric acid, watching the yellow oil fuming as he stirred in the clay mixture to soak up and render passive the incredibly sensitive and unstable nitroglycerine. It had taken three weeks to assemble the ten kilograms that now hung from *Rozinante*'s nose section.

Since they did not know of the explosive then neither, he concluded, would they surmise that the submarine was now heading towards Tórshavn.

Very slowly the craft curved towards the south-west, easing across the current that had been pushing at her stern. Now Bowman had to increase the motor speed to maintain the

165

submarine's passage. Rapidly the depth of the sea was decreasing, even though the submarine was several kilometres off-shore.

The shallow water was churning above a giant reef, the result of a tumultuous volcanic eruption at the time of the islands' formation from fissures in the deep sea. Perhaps the enormous ridge had itself once been a small island which had since been eroded away by the continuous mauling of the Atlantic. Claus had warned Bowman about the violent currents above the reef, that the submarine should not be taken too close to where the sea bed lay a mere thirty feet below the surface.

Bowman steered the boat directly west, away from the reef. His heart beat quickly for a while as a strange, sucking current dragged noisily at the hull and the depth signal changed rapidly. There was a hundred feet below the boat, then a mere forty, then a drop of over two hundred; finally it fell away more gradually.

'What was that noise?' asked Fitzgerald who had just woken.

'Reef; we were a little farther east than I estimated.' He pointed out their position on the Admiralty chart. 'That leaves us about 15 kilometres to go with half our battery charge left. It should be enough in this calm weather.'

For a few minutes they did not talk as Bowman adjusted the boat on her setting for Tórshavn to the south-west. Then he asked: 'What are you going to do when this is all over, George?'

'Have a good rest in prison, I guess. It'll come to that you know.'

'Yes, I suppose it is inevitable. If Claus does manage to pick us up, then the Fisheries' vessel is bound to catch us before we get very far.'

'"Bombs for noble causes",' intoned Fitzgerald. 'But it's still a serious crime. They're hardly going to let us get away.'

Bowman's eyes were expressionless as he stared at the screen. 'But it will hit the media with a bang; put this place on the map and show what's happening out here.' He looked out of the forward window at the device that blunted the submarine's nose. That little package was going to change everything.

'Martyrs', Willoughby had suggested. Claus understood what the fat SIS man had meant. It was too late, of course, the warning; although even if it had come earlier it would not have been heeded. To strike, immediately, before he and his friends were rendered impotent, was the only way of effecting a change to the whaling in Faroese waters. Nothing else would do it in time. This way, if they blew *Stormur* from the sea, they would buy time, and would broadcast to the world the fact that this lonely, forgotten archipelago was the centre of the last, and cruellest, large-scale whaling in the Atlantic. People needed to be shown that, and how the Norwegians and the Russians came here to hunt the last of the finbacks. They should also learn of how the Faroese trapped the great schools of *grindvhal*, and the way the beasts were slaughtered. He and Jens, and Bowman and Fitzgerald, had the means of thrusting that news on the world. What they were doing was criminal; but what established authorities, governments, were doing, or allowing to happen, was far worse than some constitutional crime.

It was one in the afternoon and Claus could see some activity on the whaler's decks.

'They are preparing to leave, Jens. As always, when they have drunk a little, Jákup leads them to the girls. When they tire of that little game we must be ready to be a bait for them.'

Poulsen was aware that he was being watched. He glanced over at the trawler. 'I see you later, bastard Dane,' he muttered. 'We sort this matter out, once and for all.' He followed his men down on to the harbour wall. Soon they had disappeared among the little house-alleys that led away from the quayside.

On board *Hannah*, Claus nodded and Jens lowered the thumper overboard. He did so on the far side of the wheelhouse from the Fisheries' vessel, so that he would not be seen by anyone watching from there. Casually, he walked over to Claus. Both men looked towards the whaler's high prows and her distinctive cannon deck which lay beneath a tarpaulin. She was quite the most remarkable boat moored in Tórshavn, lean, wickedly handsome, distinctively Norwegian in her lines.

'Can they do it, Claus; can they sink her?'

'We shall know very soon.' He glanced at his watch. 'If all goes well they will not be far away. Jákup will be with his girls now and that should keep him happy for a while.'


Bowman slept while the American watched the screen and the dazzling waters up ahead. By his reckoning they were within two kilometres of the northern tip of Nólsoy, the little island that guarded Tórshavn from the east. As yet nothing but an increasing number of fishing and ferry boats showed on the monitor screen. There was no boundary of land. Bowman had dropped the submarine down to a depth of thirty feet before he had gone to sleep. That way they would not be seen from an aeroplane passing overhead and would be safe from deep-draughted ships. There was a gentle hiss as stale air was expelled from the cabin valve, then again only the whirring motors.

Fitzgerald glanced at the lined, drawn face of the sleeping man. It was not a proper sleep, but shallow and disturbed. He wondered at the nightmares that might be passing through his companion's mind. It was good that this was to be the last dive. Neither of them could take much more, but especially not Bowman, with his continuous responsibility for the boat.

Something on the surface was rapidly approaching. Almost simultaneously Fitzgerald noticed the blip on the edge of the screen and heard the high-speed buzz of propeller screws. It was some sort of power launch. Had the submarine been sighted, or picked up on sonar? He switched their own sonar to passive. The screen was blank, but still he heard the propellers. He was on the verge of waking Bowman when he heard the sound diminishing. Switching the sonar back to active he saw that the signal was dwindling towards the edge of the screen. His heart was racing. Underwater, with a highly restricted sense of what was occurring outside, fears became concentrated. He knew how fragile the boat was; but his terrors were derived from something beyond knowledge of the mere weakness of the hull. He worried about the vessel he had heard. It could have been a fast fishing boat, or a launch, but then he rationalised that whoever was piloting it had not seen the submarine.

*Rozinante*, after all, was now entering the busiest waters around the Faroe Islands. He could no longer expect empty seas where the boat could be risked running shallow. Gradually, he opened the ballast valves until the submarine steadied at nearly forty feet as she skulked through the blue gloom, silently edging south-west.

It was half-past two when Jákup Poulsen stumbled out of the dingy building in Torgadsgøta in the east of the town. One by one his crew-men followed him on to the street. They were laughing and had obviously been drinking heavily. Singing an old whaling shanty they jigged and walked clumsily towards the harbour.

'Well, Steini,' bellowed the whaler captain, 'did you like her? What did you do to her, eh?' He clapped the little Icelander on the back and roared with laughter. 'You are a very sick man, Steini, very sick. I should not have introduced you to such a girl.' They were all laughing uncontrollably when a voice stilled the air; cold, like an iceberg on a calm sea.

'You make too much noise, Jákup.'

Wide-eyed, Poulsen turned to see the tall Dane leaning against a wall. Very slowly a smile spread on the whaler's face.

'Bastard Dane, I was just coming to visit your boat. You have saved me a walk. I fix you here.'

Claus sniffed and glanced coolly across the street to where Jens was standing, hands in his pockets. Again Poulsen laughed. 'You think he makes a difference? Two of you against Jákup, and my men; or do you have those conservationist rats hiding somewhere? Call them, eh, so that I can fix them also. You have given me too much trouble, Dane, so now I teach you how to behave. I cut you up.' From his pocket he withdrew a knife, the blade of which clicked open and gleamed.

Unblinking, Claus shook his head. 'You have no intelligence, Jákup. Hurting is all you know, all you enjoy.' As he spoke he watched carefully, taking in the fact that Poulsen had moved a little closer, almost within striking distance. But Claus had to talk, to delay the whalers from returning to *Stormur*; yet he could not forget the promise he had made to Eidi, about not hurting her brother. She had not meant that Claus could not protect himself, but he understood what she had made him vow. He saw that Jákup was a little closer, his feet shuffling imperceptibly towards him, the knife drawn back, ready to sweep. He would have to back down, to buy some more time. 'Why do you hate me so much?'

For a moment, Poulsen was rigid, like a grotesque statue. Then he spoke. 'My sister. You were with her last night.'

Claus opened his mouth to reply, but it was too late. The knife slashed through the air, catching his chin even though he had flinched backwards the second he saw the change of expression in his adversary's eyes. Instinctively, his own fist rammed into Poulsen's chest, throwing the whaler backwards.

Jens had crossed the street, already closing on the Icelander who was lifting a bottle, ready to smash it into Claus's face.

Suddenly, from down the street came a loud shout: '*Grindaboð!*' Poulsen pulled himself up and faced the man who had called. Claus, blood dripping from his chin, momentarily also looked away from his enemy. A man was running towards them. 'Jákup, Jákup,' he called. 'There are *grindvhal* in the harbour! They have arrived, at last. Come, we need you, quickly.'

As he stood up Poulsen smiled, now looking back at Claus. 'So, you are saved, bastard Dane. But maybe this will be worse. You come and watch me kill some *grindvhal*, eh? You think you

170

can stop me? Come and try; come with your damn little trawler and get in my way. I sink you, bastard. I kill you and sink your boat.' Then he had turned away and was following the man who had brought him the information he always loved to hear; that whales had been sighted. It was always best when there was a *grind* in Tórshavn, the capital. Everyone came to see the killing. Everyone could see Jákup doing what he did best; the man who had killed more *grindvhal* than any other person alive on Faroes. He would redden the waters of Tórshavn with whale blood. As he broke into a run he wondered if the sighted school was a large one.

Soon he and his men had disappeared into the town. Claus swore. 'Jens, we too have to hurry, back to *Hannah* and lift the thumper.' He glanced at his watch. It was a little past three. His friends should already have planted the mine and would be backing away from *Stormur* . . .


Nólsoy was behind them as Bowman adjusted the submarine for her final approach. The batteries had less than a quarter of their charge remaining, but it would be enough to power the boat over the last kilometre. He was nervous, adrenalin making him sensitive; there was a pain in his stomach. His hands shook and he could feel a rivulet of sweat running down his temple. He tore his attention away from the polythene-covered package that was suspended from the submarine's nose.

The boat slowed almost to a stop as Bowman examined the screen and Fitzgerald listened intently to the sounds coming through his headphones.

'We're going to have to grease her to get her through,' said the American.

'That,' said Bowman, pointing to a line on the top right of the screen, 'must be the harbour wall.' The rest of the screen was a fuzz, as conflicting signals merged, as boats criss-crossed the busy waters. 'We'll run to the south and thread her through.'

171

As *Rozinante* rounded the point of the wall, Fitzgerald abruptly lifted his arm. 'I can hear it. The thumper, due north!'

The boat swung on the tide, forty feet down in the murky harbour waters, her propellers driving her towards the sound signal. Bowman closed the vent valve from the cabin, so that there would be no tell-tale stream of bubbles on the surface.

The thumper's sound was louder. Very slowly the submarine slid beneath the moored boats. 'There,' said Fitzgerald. 'There's *Hannah*.' Bowman looked up to see the trawler's distinctive wooden curves. Up against the light he also recognised the shape of the sound device which hung down below *Hannah*. He set the course for north by north-west. Two hundred metres away *Stormur* lay at anchor with no one on board. Without hesitation, Bowman opened the motors to three quarters speed, a sudden urgency driving him. He could not stop to think now, for he knew his courage was almost exhausted. He fixed his attention up ahead, ignoring the sonar signals. The water was noisy with the sounds of propellers, and hulls slopping against the tide.

'That's odd,' came Fitzgerald's voice from apparently far away. 'I could have sworn I heard whales.' But Bowman was not listening. He was aiming at a shadow in the sea up ahead. The dark patch grew as he eased off the power to the motors. Then, the submarine was directly beneath a gaunt steel hull, *Stormur*'s hull.

Fitzgerald tapped the headphones and frowned. 'Odd,' he muttered. 'Must have been propellers.'


Dalsgaard entered Willoughby's cabin. 'The wireless operator had located another of those sound devices, directly beneath the trawler.'

The SIS Man stared coldly at the Fisheries' captain. He did not like him. Dalsgaard was apparently unprepared to take any action or responsibility without first seeking advice. It was an annoying characteristic, because otherwise Dalsgaard was an intelligent man.

'So what do you suggest we do, Captain? It is not illegal, is it, to make noises in the sea? We need more to act on than that, much more. Is the submarine here?'

'We cannot tell. Our search sonar is useless in such confined waters.' There was a knock on the door and the second officer entered the cabin.

'Sir,' he announced. 'There is a school of whales being chased into the harbour by fishing boats.'

Willoughby sighed loudly. 'Now, Captain, we will have something.' And he knew what it would be. It was obvious really; the empty whaler, the sound signal. The submarine would be down there all right and he had already worked out what load she would be carrying.

On deck Willoughby ignored the school of whales that everyone else was watching. He looked towards the moored trawler and *Stormur* and then slowly along the quayside. In the town he saw people running down towards the harbour and cars parking in the already congested roads. The Foreign Office operative would be there, having waited for just such a moment, a *grind* – Bowman and Fitzgerald were bound to reveal themselves, and there would be confusion to hide his own activities. But where would he be? Willoughby imagined where he would place himself if he had been the killer. He shook Dalsgaard by the shoulder.

'Your binoculars, Captain, quickly.'

The top of a high building, he reasoned; a sniper would have a clean shot from such a position. He scanned the highest windows and roofs of houses and shops adjacent to the harbour. He turned the binoculars towards other high structures close by; the library and museums, the academy, Hotel Hafnia. Then he looked south-west towards where the hospital stood against the skyline. Immediately he picked out a shape that was moving across the roof towards one of the ventilator shafts. He pulled down the binoculars with a jerk. That *must* be him, thought Willoughby. The killer was on the hospital roof. It would be a long shot: five hundred metres or more, but nothing to a skilled rifleman with a powerful telescopic sight.

'Captain,' he shouted, 'when Bowman or Fitzgerald show themselves get them under cover, immediately. Don't waste time by arresting them, just screen them from the hospital. There's a man with a gun up there.' He was already running down the gangway. Soon the bewildered Dalsgaard had lost sight of the fat Englishman among the crowds.

There was a loud, metallic clunk as the mine attached itself to the whaler's hull, deep beneath the bows, just aft of the cannon deck. Wide-eyed, Bowman stared at it, and at the gleaming wire that ran from the device back to a fixed ring on the submarine. His hands were poised over the motors' controls. All he had to do was reverse the electric current and the wire would be pulled free, activating the detonator timer. In five minutes the device would explode. As if in a trance, he hesitated.

'Do it, Son,' came the warm, reassuring voice of his friend.

Savagely, he turned his hands and the submarine jolted backwards. The wire was free. He felt sick as he turned the boat away.

Claus, gasping for breath after his run, heaved on the rope and dragged the sound device on board. He could see that Poulsen's men were already aboard *Stormur*, running across her deck towards the wheelhouse. Jákup himself was walking out on to the cannon deck and pulling at the tarpaulin that covered the great weapon. There was a bulge of water at the whaler's stern as her propellers span into motion.

In *Hannah*'s wheelhouse, Claus started the engine and shouted at Jens to let go the mooring ropes. He swung the helm over even as he saw *Stormur* lurch out away from the quayside. Beyond, way out by the harbour wall, was a line of fishing boats, and the distinctive white marks of whales spouting and kicking at the surface.

'The thumper, it's stopped,' said Fitzgerald suddenly.

'*Damn*; there must be someone back on board *Stormur*.' Bowman spat out the words. Without pause, he swung the submarine until she was pointing the way she had come. 'We'll have to knock the bomb off.'

'How the hell . . . There's no time?' Then they heard the sound of *Stormur*'s engines and the roar of her propellers. 'She's underway!'

The vessel approached rapidly. Bowman opened the air line in order to surface the submarine. 'We'll have to tell them,' he shouted; 'get them off that ship before the thing blows.' He turned the air valve to maximum and the boat rushed to the surface amidst a cloud of bubbles.

Poulsen saw it all happening so fast; the surface ahead mushrooming as the submarine broached, the hatch being pushed clear and the two men inside shouting; the Englishman and the American, trying to stop him going after his whales. He looked down now as *Stormur*'s bows towered above the little craft; and then the crash as steel split the glass fibre, and the look of horror on the faces of the two men as the whaler's bows crushed their boat and flung them into the cold sea, down towards the keel, and the racing, churning propeller blades. He looked towards the stern in time to see two heads surface in the wake of foam. He laughed and shouted at them. 'You are lucky, conservationist rats; my propellers miss you.' He glanced up to see the trawler rushing across the harbour. 'You try to stop me, Danes,' he roared. 'I sink you as easily as that puny boat.' His men had loaded the cannon. He patted it. 'I blow you away with my gun, eh?'

Claus watched incredulously as a column of white water shot into the air, high above *Stormur*'s superstructure, engulfing the cannon deck. A moment later came the deafening explosion as the whaler's bows were lifted from the sea. She staggered, hung and fell, and the roar of detonated nitroglycerine echoed around the harbour, and then she threw a great surge of water ahead of her as she slowed to a stop, settling by the bow amidst a cloud of smoke.

The trawler slewed around the two men in the water.

Bowman shouted frantically up at Claus: 'We're all right. Get him off. Get Poulsen off!' In under thirty seconds *Hannah* had bumped into the whaler and Claus had jumped on to the bigger ship's deck. He coughed as the dense, acrid fumes bit at his throat. It did not matter, and neither did he care about his gashed-open chin, or his stinging eyes and the blinding smoke. All he thought of was the promise he had made to Eidi; that he would not hurt Jákup. The man might already be dead, blown apart by the enormous shock of the explosion. Claus stumbled forwards, feeling his way towards the bow.

Then the smoke cleared and he could see the cannon deck, or what remained of it; a twisted mass of steaming metal, turned up from the shattered prow. The cannon itself had been turned completely around so that it faced back towards the bridge, although its nose, and the harpoon, with which it was still armed, was pointing down towards . . . Claus took it in with a feeling of desperation: the harpoon was pointing at the figure of Jákup Poulsen, lying on the distorted metal.

As the Dane stumbled over to the cannon he could hear the man sobbing, or, rather, uttering a nearly continuous groan. Most of his body was covered with bleeding cuts. His eyes looked peculiarly clear against the red marks on his face. At first they stared blankly at the sky. Then they focused on Claus's face and Jákup stopped moaning. Seeing the Dane brought him out of his hysteria. He mouthed some unintelligible words and then: 'How Claus, how?'

'A bomb, my friend, I am sorry.'

'Ah, a bomb.' His face contorted with pain. 'That was very clever.'

'It was not meant for you, just your damn boat.'

Poulsen nodded slightly. 'Your friends; they put it there?'

'We all put it there.'

'Ja, but they did it. They are more clever than you and I. But I sank them, eh?' The ship was settling rapidly. Poulsen lay just a few feet above the water. Claus pulled at some metal rigging that lay over the man's body. 'I am caught, by my own boat. You get me free, Claus; before the water reaches me.' *Stormur* juddered and Claus struggled for a hold. He wrenched at the metal, pulling it away from Poulsen's chest, but the legs were still pinned.

'I am going to have to pull you clear,' he shouted as the water slopped over the trapped man. 'It will hurt.' Even as he spoke he held Poulsen beneath the arms and pulled with all his strength. A terrible scream filled his ears and he saw a twisted hook of metal tear along one of the whaler's thighs, down to the knee where it dug in deeply. Both Poulsen's legs were under water now as the man sobbed with pain and fear. Only the hook of metal still trapped him, but it was too thick to bend by hand. Claus bunched his fingers around it, into the open leg wound, and wrenched frantically; but it would not move. The water was up to Poulsen's waist.

'The harpoon, fire the harpoon,' screamed the whaler. Claus looked at the weapon, poised above the trapped leg. *Stormur* had begun her slide, down into the harbour's depths. The water rolled along the trapped man's chest, up to his neck . . . 'Do it,' came his feverish voice. '*Fire it* . . .' A wave hit him in the face. It was the only chance. Claus jumped on to the cannon, found and twisted the grip-trigger.

After the violent crack of the nitroglycerine, the cannon's gunpowder seemed muffled, no more than a gentle thud. Diving into the water, Claus almost immediately swam into Poulsen's limp body, free now of the buckled metal of the deck. He held the man around the chest and kicked towards the surface, away from the swirling waters above the sinking ship.

He gasped for air and with a peculiar sense of relief felt the injured man choke and then fall back into unconsciousness. He could not steel himself to feel down Jákup's body for his legs. 'It is all right now. I have you safe.' He repeated the words time and time again, even when Bowman and Fitzgerald swam over to him. He refused to relinquish his grip until sailors in a launch from the Fisheries' vessel pulled Jákup to safety. He whispered, 'I have him safe, Eidi.'

Each shape in the water filled a quarter of the area of the massive object lens. The MI6 operative finely adjusted the focus until the shapes were recognisable as men's heads, close together. He settled the rifle butt into his shoulder and pressed his chin at the smooth, cold wood of the stock. He eased the weapon over until Fitzgerald's head lay framed by the cross-threads. The American first: a sighter shot at him. He squeezed the trigger and felt the familiar jolt. Unblinking he watched through the sight. A second later a spout of water kicked up at his target's shoulder. He slightly altered his position to bring Fitzgerald's image lower in the sights. Now the head – one smooth shot to finish the American; then a final shot at Bowman. His finger began to tighten over the trigger. At that moment the bows of a ship obscured his target, even as he felt the thud in his shoulder as he fired. He reloaded.

Willoughby struggled for breath as he pulled himself through the narrow doorway. Turning, he stumbled towards the prone figure at the edge of the roof. Again he ran and lifted the heavy boat-hook he had been carrying. The operative swung around and rose to his knees in time only to fire wildly, before the fat man hit him hard across the head.

In Tórshavn harbour, boats milled on the billowing waters above the wreck as the two men in the water climbed out into the Fisheries' launch. The fishing boats, far out by the harbour entrance, were also heading towards the extraordinary scene. Of the pilot whales and the submarine, as of the whaling ship, there was no longer any sign. There was a little smoke in the air, drifting north-west towards the line of distant mountains. Jákup Poulsen groaned as a sailor tightened a tourniquet to stem the flow of blood from the whaler's knee. Fitzgerald lay unconscious even as Bowman pressed a bundle of lint bandages against the shattered shoulder. Two more sailors pulled the Englishman down beneath the level of the prow.

'There is a gun-man,' one of them explained. 'You stay low please.' The speeding launch skated towards the harbour wall. Bowman struggled in their grasp, but suddenly Claus was at his side, also holding him down.

178

'It is over now. There is no more we can do, my friend. You have done what you set out to achieve. The whaling is finished.'

For attention only: Head of A Section, MI6 – Head of C Section, MI5

Ref. 3340/Counter Terrorism – Bowman, Richard; Fitzgerald, George. Directive Report from Simon Willoughby, Assistant Head of C Section, MI5.

Full cover-up procedure engaged by Foreign and Home Offices and CIA on Faroes operation. Diplomatic measures taken to ensure imminent extradition of Richard Bowman from Denmark. George Fitzgerald presently in hospital in Esbjerg under police guard. The Americans undertaking their own extradition procedures.

The trawler, *Hannah*, with Claus Hansen and Jens Petersen on board, is missing. She was last sighted off the coast of North Norway. The Danish and Norwegian Navies are conducting a search.

Willoughby paused and stared at the incomplete report on the screen. He wondered what to type next. There was no adequate explanation he could give of the extraordinary events that had concluded the affair in the Faroes. Royce, his own Head of Section, would not understand why Willoughby had interfered and changed the whole course of events out there, and the Foreign Office hierarchy would be furious.

But it was impossible to explain why men acted as they did over sensitive and emotive issues. You only understood by knowing the men, or the places in the world that drew people like Richard Bowman.

He smiled to himself as he remembered the grey-green archipelago in the cold waters of the high North Atlantic, and the strange empathy he had felt for the Danish smugglers. He knew they would evade the searching ships by hiding out in some Norwegian fjord, and he was happy with that thought.

There were men who broke laws and there were bad men; but the two were not always the same.

Nothing would be achieved by typing any more. He transmitted the report.

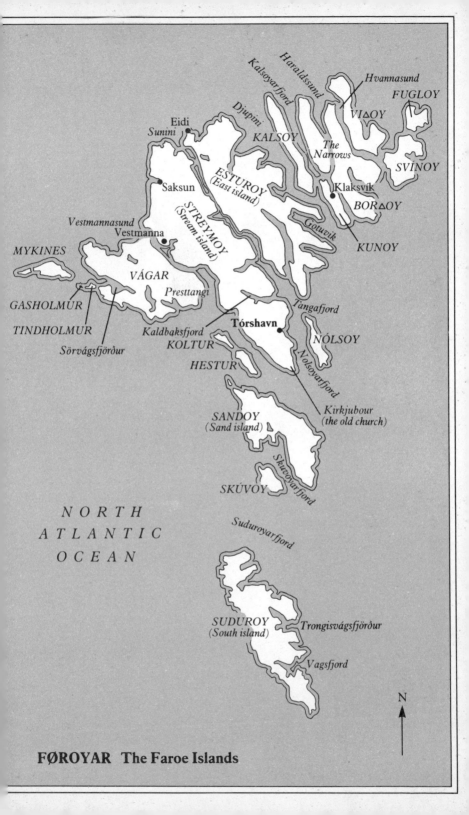

**FØROYAR** The Faroe Islands